Irish

Gardens

TERENCE REEVES-SMYTH

APPLETREE GUIDE

Published and printed by
The Appletree Press Ltd
19–21 Alfred Street
Belfast BT2 8DL
1994

British Library Cataloguing-in-Publication Data
A catalogue record for this book is
available from the British Library.

ISBN 0 86281 374 3

9 8 7 6 5 4 3 2 1

Picture Acknowledgements

Belfast Parks Department: pages 7, 8
Bord Failte: pages 12, 23, 25, 28, 49, 64, 68, 76,
83, 87
HMSO (Dept. of the Environment, Northern
Ireland): pages 30, 94
Belinda Jupp: page 92
The National Trust: pages 6, 35, 36, 38, 40, 41, 79
Office of Public Works, Dublin: page 22
Sheila Reeves-Smyth: page 11
Lord Rosse: pages 70, 73, 75

CONTENTS

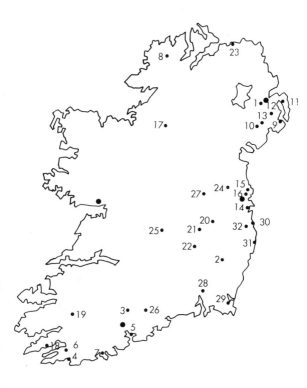

INTRODUCTION

Irish gardens attract well over half a million visitors a year, and this figure looks likely to double over the next decade as more and more people come to appreciate the intrinsic beauty, as well as the botanical and historical interest, of this significant component of Ireland's heritage. The benign climate of Ireland, particularly in the coastal regions, sustains a wide range of plants, while the country's diversity of landscape provides many opportunities for gardening, though it must be said that the real success of Irish gardens lies in the skill, patience and dedication of their owners, many of whom maintain and continually improve their gardens on their own. Indeed, a deep love of plants and a sensitivity to their needs is evident when one visits Irish gardens, and it is precisely this tradition of sympathetic planting – a tradition that has evolved over many years – that must be preserved.

The intention of this guide is to provide information on gardens that are open to the public on a regular basis. An effort has been made to include a wide range of gardens: formal gardens, Robinsonian gardens, arboreta, botanical gardens and specialised gardens, though inevitably the choice reflects both a personal taste and the constraints of this book. In each case an attempt has been made to provide some idea of the garden's history, contents and layout – enough background to give the visitor some idea of what to expect in each garden. More detailed information is normally available at the gardens themselves, though regrettably very few gardens sell detailed guides or catalogues of their plants and labelling is sometimes inadequate. Serious gardeners should find the book *Trees and Shrubs Cultivated in Ireland* by Mary Forrest an aid in their excursions (Boethius Press, 1985).

The gardens in this book are arranged alphabetically on an all-Ireland county basis. Opening times and other practical details are given at the end of each entry, as well as a National Grid Reference number (NGR) and, where relevant, an indication of the garden's best season. Gardens that are open by appointment only are not included in the main entries but are listed at the end of the book. Further information about other gardens open to the public by appointment may be obtained from Bord Failte, Baggot Street Bridge, Dublin 2 by sending a self-addressed envelope and IR £1.50. Many important Irish gardens are also only open to the public on an occasional basis, usually in support of a charity.

The County Wicklow Garden Festival, which has become an annual event in June, provides the public with the opportunity to see over fifty gardens spread over the south Leinster region – brochures are available in tourist offices. In Northern Ireland the local garden committee of the National Trust organises the opening of a small number of private gardens from spring to early autumn; leaflets listing these gardens with entry charges are available from the National Trust, Rowallane, Saintfield, County Down, BT24 7LH by sending a stamped, self-addressed envelope.

A carpet of bluebells at Rowallane

CITY OF BELFAST INTERNATIONAL ROSE GARDEN

County Antrim

Rosa *'Cherry Brandy'*

By the seventeenth century, roses were extensively grown in almost every European garden. Three hundred years later they remain firm favourites and nowhere more so than in Ulster – the home, for over a century, of two world-famous breeders: Dickson's of Newtownards and McGredy's of Portadown. It was in celebration of their achievements that the City of Belfast International Rose Garden, with its spectacular display areas, historical sections and trial beds, was established in the attractive setting of Wilmont – a landscape park of 128 acres on the east bank of the River Lagan.

An international rose trials ground was first set up at Wilmont (now known as Sir Thomas and Lady Dixon Park) between 1964 and 1965 with the backing of local government and the assistance of the newly formed Rose Society of Northern Ireland. The Rose Garden area, maintained by the Belfast City Council Parks Department, evolved gradually over the years and by the 1980s covered eleven acres, with over 20,000 roses in rectangular trial beds and larger display areas. Much of the present layout belongs to a major redevelopment of the garden that took place between 1986 and 1987.

The best time to visit the garden is during Belfast Rose Week in mid July – the period which coincides with the final judging of trial roses. The entrance approach into the garden is flanked by beds containing trial winners, while to the left a massive floribunda display covers the hill. Beyond an undistinguished stone arch lie most of the trial beds, which are regimented into a series of concentric circles and spread over the northern part of the garden. More rings of display beds are paraded in the central area of the garden and among these is a section devoted to the roses bred by the McGredy and Dickson family firms. The McGredy nursery business has produced a virtually unbroken series of floribundas, hybrid teas and climbing roses since 1895 and among their numerous award-winning successes visitors will find such familiar cultivars as 'Mischief', 'Evelyn Fison', 'Uncle Walter', 'Picadilly' and 'Molly McGredy'. Since 1972, Sam McGredy (the fourth) has continued the tradition in New Zealand, but the Dicksons are still based in Ulster where they have been breeding roses since 1879. It is this family who have given us such famous roses as 'Crimson Glory', 'Shot Silk', 'Innisfree' and the famous 'Grandpa Dickson'. Today the Dickson family mostly produce floribundas, patio roses and shrub roses, rather than the classical hybrid roses of the past.

A display garden tracing the history of the rose can be found close to Wilmont House. It is laid out in the form of a spiral path, with the oldest roses on the outside leading to modern hybrid roses in the centre. Roses are a very complex group of plants and this simplistic layout, which lacks many important cultivars, is quite disappointing.

Other attractions of the park include an international camellia trials ground south west of the house. The trials usually take place in early April and the camellias may be found inside and outside the east side of the Walled Garden. The park also contains some fine trees, a selection of azaleas and rhododendrons, an icehouse, a yew walk and an attractive but recently damaged bamboo walk. West of the latter lies a large but unexceptional area that purports to be a Japanese garden.

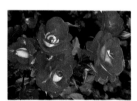

Rosa *'Molly McGredy'*

Located 1½ miles south east of Dunmurry on the Upper Malone Road, Belfast. NGR: J 307677. Open daily, all year. Walled garden: weekdays, 8.00 am – 4.00 pm; weekends, 2.00 – 4.00 pm. Refreshments available in stables. Toilet facilities. Suitable for wheelchairs. Dogs on lead. Admission: free. Best season: April to August.

ALTAMONT

County Carlow

Some of the most beautiful gardens are those which manage a successful transition between formal areas around the house and informal and wild parts beyond. At Altamont the plush lawns, box hedging and clipped yews merge almost imperceptibly with the lake below, where skilled and artistic planting has created delightful all-season effects. Paths beyond lead to lovely woodlands, an arboretum, a bog garden and, down a magic Ice Age ravine, to the majestic wooded banks of the River Slaney.

Part of the fascination of Altamont is its complex history. The central portion of the house was built by the St George family in the 1770s, incorporating an earlier building which may include portions of a medieval nunnery. The early house faced north, but after the building of a new road to the east it was reversed and new avenues laid down with handsome gates and surrounding beech plantations. These remain unchanged, but the area to the north was dramatically altered during the 1840s by the Dawson Borrer family who had by then acquired the property. Using the abundant labour available during the Famine, a large lake was dug, terraced lawns created and a central broad walk extended down to the lake with flanking yews and beds. In the early part of the present century the property was acquired by Feilding Lecky Watson, a plantsman with a keen interest in rhododendrons which he grew from seeds acquired through sponsorship of Himalayan expeditions, such as those of Kingdon Ward's, and through exchanges with other gardens. After his death in 1943 the garden slid into genteel ossification, but since the 1970s his daughter and present owner, Mrs Corona North, has embarked on a major programme to revitalise and transform the gardens. The lake has been dredged, the walks cleared, new areas created, such as the Bog Garden, and a wide-ranging collection of plants have been added.

Upon arriving visitors pass the bowed front of the house, whose mellow-coloured façade is covered with a venerable wisteria and *Parthenocissus henryana*. On the east wing stands a beautiful thirty-foot-high *Rhododendron augustinii*, one of the finest of all rhododendrons and named after Augustine Henry, the Irish customs official and plant collector. To the left of the hall door, amidst a variety of lush planting, is a fine specimen of the fragrant *Clerodendrum trichotomum fargesii* – a present to Altamont from Lord Rosse around 1960 and noted for its bright blue berries in autumn.

From the car park the visitor approaches the gardens through an antique iron gate, passing the tea room and a little courtyard opposite filled with plants, including a thriving *Myrtus apiculata* 'Glanleam Gold'. A small gate beyond leads onto the beech-lined Nun's Walk whose origins may go back as early as the seventeenth century. In the shade of the trees to the right, flanked by aromatic skimmas, lies the entrance to the garden centre and nursery in the Walled Garden. Further down the walk a path to the left, leading to the formally laid out beds in front of the house, passes beneath a spreading *Parrotia persica* whose leaves turn a lovely crimson gold in autumn.

Flanked on either side by substantial beds, a rectangular goldfish pond shimmers directly below the perron in dramatic alignment with the central walk to the lake. The bed on the right, bordered with box hedging, contains a collection of dwarf conifers and shrubs underplanted with heathers and bulbs. Plants here include *Picea koraiensis*, grown from seed brought from Peking, a specimen of *Abies koreana* and the Irish dwarf pine *Pinus sylvestris* 'Hibernica'. The opposite bed contains a wealth of plants: golden bays (*Laurus nobilis* 'Aurea'), a silver-variegated dogwood (*Cornus alterifolia* 'Argentea') and the tree peony *P. lutea ludlowee* – a splendid variety brought back from Tibet by Kingdon Ward. There are also choice buddleias and willows, aromatic French lavender and a variety of perennials, notably the variegated brunnera, the deep-purple-leaved heuchera and foxtail lilies, whose stately spires always make a great show in summer. Here too are clumps of the Irish-bred *Primula* 'Garryarde Guinevere' first shown in Dublin in 1935 and distinguished by its yellow-eyed purple-pink flowers and its fine bronze foliage.

The central broadwalk down to the lake is flanked by clipped Irish yews and box-hedged beds framing roses that are underplanted with daffodils and tulips for spring colour. Modern floribunda and hybrid tea roses occupy the top beds, while further down old-fashioned varieties predominate, such as the richly fragrant Damask rose 'Mme Hardy' and the gorgeous light pink Alba rose 'Céleste'. Across the lawn to the left is a little octagonal pool shadowed by a large *Magnolia stellata* and beyond, a fine fern-leaf beech probably planted around the 1840s. An equally old

View across the lake at Altamont

holm oak dignifies the area, while other fine trees along this side of the garden include a yew at least three-centuries old, a sweetly scented balsam poplar and adjacent to the lake, a venerable *Prunus* 'Ukon' with unusual creamy-green flowers.

The lake-side planting beyond the sundial proffers quite a variety of moisture-loving plants, including a good selection of hostas, candelabra primulas, astilbes, gunnera, hydrangeas, saxifrages and some blue poppies, such as the Kingdon Ward variety *Meconopsis betonicifolia*. In this area striking specimens of the swamp cypress *Taxodium distichum* and the rarer *T. ascendens*, as well as a Kilmacurragh cypress and a dawn redwood, flourish.

To the right of the sundial a lovely pocket handkerchief tree and a tulip tree, both planted thirty years ago, reward the eye. Close by is a splendid *Rhododendron cinnabarinum* with scented tubular flowers of terra-cotta orange, planted in 1917. The path here to the Azalea Walk passes a border of peonies underplanted with orange tiger lilies, cyclamens and colchicums for seasonal colour. At the bridge another old rhododendron branches forward – an unnamed arboreum cultivar with pink-red flowers and black freckles.

The walk along the opposite shore of the lake past the Myshall Gate leads to the statue of a little boy; here another tributary path brings the visitor to the new arboretum. This lush allotment contains a good collection of Chilean species, including *Eucryphia glutinosa*, *Drimys winteri*, *Embothrium coccineum* 'Longifolium' and varieties of *Nothofagus*. After a diversion to a bog garden further down, the path winds through a glen of ancient mossy oak woods to the River Slaney where visitors will find themselves treading on carpets of bluebells and wild daffodils in the spring. The path along the river and up the mid nineteenth-century granite 100 Steps (and there are one hundred steps!) leads across a field back to the house, passing a Wellingtonia that was once surrounded by a crown of Portugal laurel – probably planted in 1866 to commemorate the fiftieth anniversary of the battle of Waterloo.

Located 5 miles south of Tullow on the Bunclody Road (N80/81). Signposted. NGR: S 890648. Open Easter to October every Sunday and bank holiday: 2.00 – 6.00 pm; other days by appointment. Home-made teas available. Garden centre. Partly suitable for wheelchairs. No dogs. Admission: adults IR £2.00; children under 10 free. Midweek and weekend residential gardening courses are held during the summer months. Tel: (0503) 59128.

Herbaceous borders in Annes Grove

ANNES GROVE

County Cork

There are few gardens anywhere in Ireland where rare trees and shrubs are grown so successfully and in such a harmonious setting as the beautiful Robinsonian garden of Annes Grove. Set on a sloping site around an elegant early eighteenth-century house overlooking the River Awbeg, the thirty-acre garden is filled with thousands of thriving plants in a layout that merges unobtrusively into the landscape. In front of the house stretches a parkland with some fine trees; nearby is a walled garden with herbaceous borders, yew walk, rock garden and water garden; beyond is an extensive woodland garden noted for its rhododendrons; and down below in a wooded limestone gorge is a lovely river garden with an island, stony rapids, rustic bridges and a lush tapestry of green foliage.

Some trees still survive at Annes Grove from the formal layout associated with the early eighteenth-century house, then known as Ballyhemock, that Lieutenant-General Grove Annesley built here on land he had inherited from the Grove family. The informal park was created in the late eighteenth century, but after this date only minor alterations occurred at Annes Grove until 1900 when Richard Grove Annesley (1879–1966) came of age and inherited the property. Over the next sixty years he was to develop Annes Grove into one of the great gardens of Ireland.

Richard Grove Annesley's interest in gardening may have originally stemmed from visits to Castlewellan where his cousin, the fifth Earl of Annesley, had created one of the greatest arboreta of the age; but it was his lifelong friendship with the fourth Marquis of Headford, one of the great garden enthusiasts of his time, that encouraged Grove Annesley to develop his knowledge of plants. Headford was a personal friend and patron of the plant collector George Forrest, and following his example Grove Annesley joined in the sponsorship of plant hunting expeditions to the Himalayas and beyond. Seeds collected by Forrest and Kingdon Ward, notably rhododendrons, duly arrived back at Annes Grove, and these together with numerous plants exchanged with other gardens were used to create a garden in the 'wild' style initiated by William Robinson – the eminent Irish gardener and writer who advocated suiting the garden to the terrain and the plant to the location. After the death of Grove Annesley in 1966, the formidable task of maintaining the gardens fell upon his son, the late E. P. Grove Annesley, and are now being successfully conserved by his grandson, Patrick Grove Annesley, the present owner of Annes Grove.

The visitor will first notice the Victorian plantings. Along the avenue are some fine mature trees, including an *Abies magnifica* from California at least sixty-six-feet high and a Japanese Yezo spruce (*Picea jezoensis*) some fifty-feet tall. Close to the house is a fine *Cedrus deodara* from the Himalayas underplanted with cyclamen, a huge *Rhododendron ponticum* and a variety of interesting shrubs, many from South America, bordering a spacious lawn. The house front itself is covered with the evergreen *Euonymus fortunei* and the deciduous *Actinidia chinensis*, notable for its heart-shaped leaves and cup-shaped white flowers in summer.

The Walled Garden, formerly devoted to kitchen produce, was transformed by Richard Grove Annesley in 1907 into a large ornamental garden. He laid a path across the allotment, focusing upon a Victorian summer house that stands on a mound, and along this path made a lovely double herbaceous border backed with yew hedges. In fact, the building is off-centre from the path – a miscalculation that is concealed by the presence, at the end, of a pair of Lawson cypresses (*Chamaecyparis* 'Erecta Viridis'). The creation of this path, which crossed the old axial path through the garden, helped to divide the area up into a number of separate compartments – each developed individually by Grove Annesley. Within these compartments he created a small rose garden, the box-edged 'Ribbon beds' filled with annuals – notably mixed petunias, a pergola with vines, honeysuckle, clematis and rambling roses – and a series of borders containing perennials and shrubs. The most astonishing feature here, however, is the Water Garden. Laid out around a serpentine pool, it proffers a wealth of aquatic and marginal plants: hostas, rodgersias, libertias, sagittarias, nymphaeas as well as irises, astilbes and bergenias – all contributing to an almost tropical atmosphere in this secluded part of the garden.

From the wild garden in miniature, the visitor proceeds on to the rather larger, wild Woodland Garden. This is approached along the Dublin Drive, laid down in 1854, where the elegant white-flowering dogwood *Cornus kousa chinensis* flourishes. It has been suggested that this shrub may be one of the original introductions of the plant from China in 1907. Further down the drive, passing honaria, pieris and *Myrtus apiculata* shrubs, the visitor enters the Rhododendron Garden which was begun in 1906 when Grove Annesley discovered an area of acidic soil. Most of the rhododendrons are species rather than hybrids and many come from seed introduced from China and the Himalayas by Kingdon Ward. They range in size and colour from whites to blues to reds, with many fine *R. cinnabarinum* and *R. griersonianum*. From the Woodland Garden there is a winding path down into the gorge, passing fine specimens of Wilson and Watson magnolias, a drooping *Juniperus recurva* 'Castlewellan' and a large *Azara microphylla*, one of a number of fine azaras intermixed with rhododendrons in these woods.

The Water Garden in the gorge was begun in 1902 when Richard Grove Annesley employed a battalion of soldiers from the nearby barracks of Fermoy to divert the Awbeg River so that it flowed closer to the house. They created an island, built weirs and rapids and later constructed bridges to span the river. Statuesque conifers were planted in the glen and screens of bamboo encouraged by the waterside together with gunnera, day lilies, polygonums, phormiums, rodgersias and astilbes. Among the primula cultivars that line the riverside walks is a huge bed of *Primula florindae*. This giant cowslip variety, with large heads of pendant, bell-shaped, sulphur-yellow flowers, was introduced by Frank Kingdon Ward in the 1920s and named after Richard Grove Annesley's wife, Florinda. It remains one of the showpieces of this quite remarkable garden.

Located 10 miles north west of Fermoy and 2 miles north of Castletownroche. NGR: R 682048. Open 17 March to 30 September: weekdays and Saturdays, 10.00 am – 5.00 pm; Sundays, 1.00 – 6.00 pm. Groups by appointment at any time. Lunches by special arrangement. Picnics. Partly suitable for wheelchairs. Dogs on lead. Admission: adults IR £2.00; senior citizens and students IR £1.50; children IR £1.00. Reductions for pre-booked groups. Tel: (022) 26145.

CREAGH

County Cork

Those in search of a romantic garden with an intimate, reposeful ambience will surely find Creagh very much to their taste. This is a delightful, informal garden set in the wooded grounds of an old demesne that extends down to the shore of a river estuary. Acquired by Gwendoline and Peter Harold-Barry at the end of the last war, the garden has been developed by both of them, making excellent use of existing features, notably a mill pond and the ruins of a mill house. An extensive network of tracks and paths meander their way through the woodlands, across glades and along the strand, enabling the visitor to view a wide range of tender plants. These include camellias, azaleas, rhododendrons, fuchsias, magnolias, telopeas and abutilons – all enjoying the gentle climate of West Cork.

The focus of the garden is a very pleasant Regency house, circa 1820, with wide eaves and a deep semicircular bow. From the lawns in front of the house, the visitor follows a straight gravel walk leading down to the pier. A short distance to the left, a narrow path through woodland winds around a serpentine mill pond amidst a scene reminiscent of a Henri Rousseau landscape – from which the garden was inspired. The waters of the pond and mill race contain arum lilies while their banks support much exotic foliage, including the prickly rhubarb *Gunnera manicata* whose leaves unfurl into huge impressive umbrellas. Other plantings comprise the New Zealand cabbage tree *Cordyline australis* and the New Zealand flax *Phormium tenax*, both of which are conspicuous features of gardens in this part of Ireland. The tree fern *Dicksonia antarctica* is also native of New Zealand, while varieties of hydrangeas provide colour along Creagh's waterside in late summer.

Passing the octagonal folly-like ruins of the old mill house with its mysterious Gothic openings peering out through the undergrowth, the path winds on through a woodland glade filled with a variety of rhododendrons. A turning to the right leads into an old walled garden, half of which is devoted to growing kitchen garden produce – vegetables, herbs and fruit – while the remainder is used to keep exotic varieties of fowl. A path from here guides the visitor out to a long south-facing border on the woodland fringe containing a variety of shrubs and interesting old roses. Returning back through the woods, the visitor will pass the site of a large Edwardian rosary in front of the house where a good range of tender fuchsias can be seen leaning against the terrace wall. Depending on time available, the visitor has the option from here of taking many more routes through the garden – indeed, be prepared to spend the best part of an afternoon in this heady and fragrant place.

Located 3½ miles south of Skibbereen on the Baltimore Road. NGR: W 077312. Open daily, all year: 10.00 am – 6.00 pm. Suitable for wheelchairs. Sorry, no dogs. Admission: adults IR £1.50; children IR £0.75. Tel: (028) 22121. Best season: April to June.

FOTA ISLAND ARBORETUM

County Cork

Few arboreta give so much pleasure and interest as Fota – home of a world-famous collection of trees and shrubs. Forming part of the ornamental grounds of a splendid Regency mansion, this arboretum together with a water garden, rock garden and a walled Italian garden is filled with plants from all over the world, especially Chinese and South American species, and benefits enormously from a mild and sheltered micro-climate. A magnificent demesne park surrounds the house and gardens and occupies the whole of the 780-acre Fota (or Foaty) Island, situated in one of the many inlets of Cork Harbour and skirted by rail and road connections from Cork to Cobh.

The gardens at Fota were begun in 1825 after John Barry-Smith, a desce. dant of the Earls of Barrymore who held this island from the twelfth century, commissioned Richard Morrison and his son Vitruvius to transform an old hunting box into his principal Irish residence. The Morrisons were responsible for the ancillary buildings and probably also helped with the garden layout and demesne park, whose surrounding walls and plantations were largely created at this time. The spreading lawns and Walled Garden, with its rusticated piers and wrought-iron gates, belong to John Barry-Smith's time, but it was his son James Hugh Barry-Smith who was responsible for creating the famous arboretum in the 1840s. He constructed the Fernery and the Water Garden by reclaiming a large area of boggy ground, and the Orangery and Temple soon followed. James Hugh disliked the damp climate, however, and spent much of his time away from Ireland, but his son Arthur who became the first (and last) Lord Barrymore devoted himself to Fota; with the help of his gardener William Osbourne, he laid the basis of the famous collection of trees and shrubs that it now contains. Lord Barrymore's work was continued by his son-in-law and daughter, Major and Honourable Mrs Dorothy Bell, who continued planting here until the late 1960s, adhering faithfully to old gardening traditions.

Amongst the original plantings at Fota is a marvellous Lebanese cedar planted in 1825 and undercarpeted with cyclamen. It stands on the lawn opposite the gate to the Walled Garden, where a magnificent specimen of *Magnolia grandiflora* 'Goliath' shades a charming little temple. The magnolias are one of Fota's special features, its most famous specimen a seventy-five-foot tall *M. campbellii* planted in 1872 which bears beautiful large pink flowers and traditionally said to be at its loveliest on St Patrick's Day. Other magnolias among the twelve species in the gardens include some rare hybrids, such as *M. x thompsoniana*, thought to be the first hybrid magnolia to be raised in western Europe.

The Fernery, essentially a large rockery planted with smaller ferns, saxifrages and Solomon's seal with huge fronds of *Dicksonia antarctica* hanging overhead, is a lush, green haven. Though not part of the arboretum, it is worth visiting, as is the pond with its little island and bordering of arum and white and pink lilies floating on the surface.

It is the trees at Fota, however, which distinguish this garden above all. A towering *Sequoia* seems to dominate the whole arboretum, while beautiful weeping spruces, silver firs, a *Drimys winteri* (which is said to have originated from seed collected by Elwes in the Andes in 1902), a colossal fern-leafed beech, massive lomatias and exceptional specimens of melaleuca and pseudopanax also take pride of place. Shooting upwards, a *Phyllocladus trichomanoides* from New Zealand, planted in 1941, is now twenty-two-feet high, the tallest in the British Isles. And a *Cryptomeria japonica* 'Spiralis', planted in 1852 just ten years after its introduction, is the tallest of its kind in Europe. Here also is a huge *Parrotia persica* dating from 1902, a *Torreya californica* planted in 1852 and now thirty-five-feet high, a large and very striking *Davidia involuc-*

rata vilmoriniana from China, and a charming *Dacrydium franklinii* from Tasmania, planted in 1855 and now, at twenty-eight feet, the largest in the British Isles. At every turn the visitor will encounter superb specimens and any passion for trees should be fully indulged.

Sadly the whole future of this remarkable garden and arboretum is now in serious jeopardy. In 1975 the house and demesne were sold to University College Cork and were subsequently resold, in 1990, to a foreign development company who have recently received planning permission to build a leisure complex on the island, incorporating hotels, golf courses and numerous glorified bungalows. Damaging tree clearance has already taken place in the arboretum; at the time of writing over 300 'overmature' trees were in the process of being felled in the park – a popular excuse in Ireland to justify the felling of hardwoods over one hundred-years old. Should this devastation continue, the beauty and tranquillity of Fota will be forever lost.

Located 9 miles east of Cork city on the Cobh Road. NGR: W 790715. Open daily, April to September: weekdays and Saturdays, 10.00 am – 6.00 pm; Sundays, 11.00 am – 6.00 pm. October: weekends, 11.00 am – 6.00 pm. Parking beside arboretum. Refreshments at wildlife park. Gift shop. Toilet facilities in car park. Suitable for wheelchairs. Dogs on lead. Admission: free for arboretum; parking IR £1.50 per car. Tel: (021) 812728.

ILNACULLIN
(GARINISH ISLAND)

County Cork

Celebrated gardens rarely live up to their reputations so effortlessly as Ilnacullin, alias Garinish – an enchanted garden island lying in a sheltered inlet of Bantry Bay. Blessed with spectacular sea and mountain scenery as well as a balmy climate brought by the equatorial waters of the Gulf Stream, this thirty-seven-acre island has a seductive mixture of formal and informal gardens superbly filled with a rich and wonderful variety of plant forms and colour.

Ilnacullin, the 'island of holly', was no more than a barren rock covered with furze and heather, surmounted by a Martello tower, when it was purchased in 1910 from the War Office by John Annan Bryce (1874–1924), a Belfast businessman and Scottish MP. Bryce commissioned the English architect and horticulturalist Harold Peto (1854–1933) to design a garden on the island. From 1911 to 1914 over one hundred men were engaged in moving soil, blasting rocks, planting trees, laying paths, as well as building a walled garden, a tall clock tower and a wonderful Italianate garden complete with casita, pool and pavilion. Peto's use of Italian Renaissance architecture and his adaptation of the picturesque formal style of gardening, made popular by the famous Lutyens and Jekyll partnership, proved to be brilliantly successful in this island setting, although it was nearly a generation later before his work would be fully appreciated. Strong winds damaged much of the early planting and it was not until the outstanding Scottish gardener Murdo Mackenzie was put in charge of the garden in 1928 that the problem was solved. Mackenzie successfully established shelter belts, mostly Scots and Monterey pine, and then proceeded to build up the splendid collection of rare and tender plants for which the island is now famous. After ownership of the island passed from the Bryce family to the Office of Public Works in 1953, Mackenzie remained in charge, retiring in 1971. His remarkable work at Ilnacullin stands as one of the great success stories of Irish horticulture.

Boats bringing visitors to sample the delights of Ilnacullin pass basking seals on the journey and arrive at the north side of the island. The route from here up to the Italian gardens winds past some outstanding plants. Of particular note is a tall and attractive example of the pendulous Australian wattle (*Acacia pravissima*). On the left is a fine *Crinodendron hookeranum* whose long crimson lanterns hang thickly from its branches in summer, while opposite an *Abutilon* 'Ashford Red' with glorious strawberry-red flowers must be the envy of most visiting gardeners. Also from Chile is a fine specimen of *Desfontainea spinosa*, which some may mistake for holly were it not for its striking orange-yellow tubular flowers. Close by a hardy but rare Chinese shrub (*Stachyurus chinensis*) branches out, while also along this path, amidst a variety of magnolias, camellias and fuchsias, is a fine specimen of the tender Kauri pine (*Agathis australis*) with its exotic-looking thick-spreading branches.

Without warning the visitor suddenly arrives in the wisteria-covered colonnades of the Italian Garden Casita. This marvellous building of Bath stone, which once housed Bryce's collection of old master drawings, gazes down over a formal sunken garden featuring a reflecting pool, a pavilion and the distant landscape beyond. This view has appeared on so many chocolate boxes and calendars that it should be familiar to most visitors, though it never fails to please. The varied planting here includes a selection of fuchsias, camellias, myrtles and scented rhododendrons, tender abutilons and cestrums, a variety of magnificent sun-loving callistemons and unusually large leptospermum shrubs, including the pink-flowering manuka (*Leptospermum scoparium* 'Nicholas II'). There are also examples of the fragrant yellow-flowering and curiously attractive 'wire-netting' bush *Corokia cotoneaster* and the tropical South American shrub *Cassia corymbosa*. Arranged in pots around the pool is a venerable collection of bonsai specimens, including a larix said to be 300-years old.

From the Casita a path winds south through more exotic plantings, including a fine specimen of the New Zealand shrub *Pseudowintera colorata* whose leathery, aromatic leaves are coloured yellow-green and dark crimson underneath. Shooting upwards is an example of the rarely seen Toatoa pine (*Phyllocladus glaucus*), with varieties of embothrium, lomatia, stranvaesia and pieris beneath. From here the visitor emerges onto a long, grassy vista known as the Happy Valley delimited on either side by impressive outcrops of rock, some of which have rambling roses trained over them. At one end a small, roofless Grecian temple surmounted on a terrace overlooks the sea, while at the bottom of the valley lies a lily pond with canes of the bamboo

Arundinaria japonica attractively overhanging it. Along the course of the valley is quite a varied collection of trees and shrubs, including an example of the pendulous *Dacrydium franklinii* and a very tall specimen of the New Zealand rimu (*Dacrydium cupressinum*). There are some particularly magnificent rhododendrons along the east end of the valley together with the evergreen *Lyonothamnus floribundus asplenifolius* from California and an example of *Chamaecyparis lawsoniana* 'Ellwoodii' that has grown remarkably tall in the island's balmy conditions.

Main herbaceous border in walled garden at Ilnacullin

A broad flight of steps leads up to the Martello tower, built in 1805 on the highest point of the island; here one has a delightful panorama of the whole garden and landscape beyond. From the tower the path leads downhill to a walled kitchen garden dominated by a tall folly built in one corner. The main path, with attractive matching gates at each end, is flanked by wide herbaceous borders brimming with varieties of aster, phlox, campanula, dianthus, centaurea, delphinium and erigeron. A cross-path focuses upon a Roman sarcophagus where a specimen of *Michelia doltsopa* thrives. The attractive stone and brick walls of the garden support a fine collection of climbing plants, but sadly the garden's perimeter paths are no longer properly maintained and access is denied to visitors.

From the Walled Garden one emerges into the old tennis court area, lushly bedded with many tender plants including varieties of grevillea, olearia, magnolia, rhododendron, viburnum, azara, fuchsia, camellia and ceanothus. A large expanse of lawn between this area and the Casita provides some relief from the dense planting of the island and is a peaceful place to relax in after journeying through the gardens. There is no tea house on the island, so visitors should come with a plentiful picnic and be prepared to spend much of the day in this enchanted place. It should be noted that the exorbitant boat fares to the island do not include admission charges into the garden, which are modest.

Located on an island in Bantry Bay, near Glengarriff. NGR: V 935550. Open daily, March and October: weekdays and Saturdays, 10.00 am – 4.30 pm; Sundays, 1.00 – 5.00 pm. April to June, September: weekdays and Saturdays, 10.00 am – 6.30 pm; Sundays, 1.00 – 7.00 pm. July and August: weekdays and Saturdays, 9.30 am – 6.30 pm; Sundays, 11.00 am – 7.00 pm. Toilet facilities. Admission: adults IR £1.50; children and students IR £0.60; groups and senior citizens IR £1.00 (group rates apply to groups of 20+ and where payment is made in one transaction). Travel is by boat (IR £4.00 return), landings one hour before closing times. Tel: (027) 63040.

The Italian garden casita, Ilnacullin

TIMOLEAGUE

County Cork

Some of the most varied and profuse gardens are those that have been developed over many generations. At Timoleague no less than five successive generations have left their mark on these charming and informal gardens on the banks of the Argideen River. Colour and interest is further enlivened by a good display of frost-tender plants which thrive in the mild and moist climate of this part of Ireland.

Visitors arrive at a car park just inside the front gates, close to the site of old Timoleague House. This was an imposing late Georgian building which for a century was the focal point of the gardens, built by Colònel Robert Travers after he purchased the demesne in 1818 from creditors of the seventh Earl of Barrymore. Unfortunately, Timoleague was burnt in 1920 during the Troubles; the Travers family subsequently built a new house in 1926 close to the ruins of the thirteenth-century Barry castle.

A long terraced lawn, originally designed between 1873 and 1874 as the home of a local tennis club, separates the site of the old house from the new. Some of the most interesting plants in the garden are to be found at the south end of this lawn, close to the old house site. Here the visitor will come across a collection of spring-flowering azaleas and magnolias together with some fine mature trees, including an example of the very attractive maple *Acer cappadocicum* 'Rubrum' and the smoke tree (*Cotinus coggygria* 'Foliis Purpureis'), whose marvellous plum-purple leaves change to lovely light shades in the autumn. A pleasing find is the shapely *Crytomeria japonica* 'Elegans', a beautiful variety of cedar with a tall, bushy habit that often succumbs to the windy Irish weather. An unusually large example of a Monterey cypress grows close by as does a foxglove tree, *Paulownia tormentosa*, and species of the Australian evergreen *Pittosporum*, all of which do particularly well in this mild seaside climate.

The avenue bank is lined with evergreens and carpeted with cyclamen in autumn. At the top lies a recently restored sunken garden with formal beds and a lily pond. Here visitors will see specimens of the New Zealand cabbage tree (*Cordyline australis*) and the tall grey-leaved, bright yellow-flowering Moroccan broom (*Cytisus battandieri*). Above, steps overhung with a lime arch lead up to the Lower Garden where a long double herbaceous border positively thrives: *Hydran-*

gea aspera, crimson-flowering *Rosa moyesii* and the lush, sun-loving Australian 'bottle-brush' (*Callistemon linearis*) all grow in profusion here. The early nineteenth-century Walled Garden lies past the greenhouses where a variety of fruit and vegetables are grown. On the way back, the visitor should enter the River Garden that is now being developed on the banks of the Argideen, beyond the ruins of the medieval castle.

Located in Timoleague, 8 miles south of Bandon and 11 miles south west of Kinsale. NGR: W 471439. Open daily, Easter weekend and mid May to mid September: 12.00 – 6.00 pm. Picnic site and children's playground. Toilet facilities. Suitable for wheelchairs. Dogs on lead. Admission: adults IR £1.50; children IR £0.75. Groups by prior arrangement. Tel: (023) 46116 or (021) 831512.

Hypericum calycinum, *or the Rose of Sharon*

GLENVEAGH CASTLE GARDENS

County Donegal

The rugged Donegal highlands may be one of the bleakest places in Ireland, but in a secluded valley beside a mountain lough is a most remarkable garden. Laid out around the operatic setting of a baronial castle, this ten-acre garden comprises formal and informal areas with a wealth of vegetation, almost tropical in its luxuriance and brimming with rare and tender plants.

The garden was begun in the 1870s by Mrs Adair, a rich American heiress, following the construction of Glenveagh Castle on a bare hillside. After her death in 1929 the property was acquired by Mr Kingsley Porter, Professor of Art at Harvard, and later in 1937 by another American, Henry P. McIlhenny, once described by Andy Warhol as 'the only person in Philadelphia with glamour'. Although he only spent three months at Glenveagh each year, McIlhenny invested huge sums improving and enlarging the garden, much of it following the advice of the landscape designer Lanning Roper and the great plantsman James Russell. Most of the major work was finished by 1967, but McIlhenny continued to introduce new plants until 1983 when he gave the castle and its gardens to the nation to form the centre-piece of a 28,000-acre National Park that had been established in 1975.

Tantalising glimpses of the castle greet the visitor along the winding lough shore road from the heather-roofed reception centre. The journey is two miles and should be walked for a full appreciation of Glenveagh's magnificent landscape setting. The starting point of a walk around the gardens, however, must begin with the Pleasure Ground to the north of the castle. This comprises a broad sweep of level lawn with bordering trees and shrubs planted to resemble the shape of the adjacent lough. The large tree rhododendrons and Scots pine, planted over a century ago, provide the area with shelter and help to create a micro-climate that is suit-able for growing a range of tender plants. Among these are some large examples of the tree fern *Dicksonia antarctica*. The condition favours rapid growth and visitors may note a tall *Pseudopanax crassifolius* from New Zealand (planted in 1971) and a large and very beautiful *Magnolia tripetala*. Along the lawn edges are drifts of astilbes, alchemillas, candelabra primulas, agapanthus and meconopsis, in addition to azaleas, *Olearia semidentata*, *Michelia doltsopa* and *Lomatia hirsuta*. There are also Japanese maples, notably an exceptional specimen of *Acer palmatum* 'Atropurpureum'.

Colour is all important. One of the border shrubs in the Pleasure Ground, *Senecio greyi*, was planted by McIlhenny for its lovely grey foliage – he hated its yellow blooms which he had removed each year. Nearby a mass of white arum lilies (*Zantedeschia aethiopica*) grow beneath a pink *Rhododendron kyawi*, both of which flower at exactly the same time providing a wonderful colour contrast in early summer. Not all the blossom is confined to the border edges – visitors leaving at the head of the garden should remember to look up to see the myriad blooms of the snowdrop tree, *Styrax japonica*.

Running above the Pleasure Ground to the Walled Garden is the Belgian Walk, laid down in 1915 by Belgian soldiers who were convalescing here during the war. Giant-leaved rhododendrons thrive in this area, along with delicate varieties of *R. edgworthii* and the white-scented *R.* 'Lady Alice Fitzwilliam'. A stone-flagged Italian terrace along this walk comes as a surprise. Although only built in 1966, it has an air of timeless serenity with its antique Italian sculpture and massed terracotta pots of various sizes planted with Ghent azaleas and hostas.

The formal Walled Garden beside the castle provides a striking contrast to the informal planting elsewhere. It is divided into squares and contains, in addition to herbaceous borders, a mixture of fruit, vegetables and flowers in the *jardin potager* style. The vegetables, many of which are grown for their foliage, are planted in bold and clearly labelled blocks. At the lower end clipped box hedges lead to the frame of a fine Gothic orangery erected to a design by Philippe Jullian. The herbaceous borders contain fairly traditional plants – yellow loosestrife, lamb's ears, catmint, phloxes, delphiniums, irises and geraniums.

A flight of steps from the *potager* cross-path leads to the View Garden and the Swiss Walk, both of which offer lovely vistas of the landscape beyond the gardens. From here a path reaches the castle terrace and the Italian Garden – a rectangular grass enclosure with tightly clipped griselinia hedges and a pair of *Acer pseudoplatanus* 'Leopoldii' shading statues.

There is much else to see at Glenveagh and visitors will probably want to spend the whole day here even if

Glenveagh Castle and its dramatic landscape setting

it is raining. It's sad that parts of this enchanting garden are closed to the public, including the astonishing, almost vertical stone staircase of sixty-seven steps leading to the upper terrace and overlooking the lough and distant mountains.

Located 15 miles north west of Letterkenny, outside of Churchill. NRG: C 021210. Open daily, Easter to last Monday in October: 10.30 am – 6.30 pm. Sundays in June, July, August: 10.30 am – 7.30 pm. Other times by arrangement. Access to garden by OPW minicoaches only. Parking at Visitor Centre. Refreshments and meals available. Toilet facilities. Admission: adults IR £1.50; senior citizens and groups IR £1.00; students and children IR £0.60. Tel: (074) 37088/37090/37262.

CASTLE WARD

County Down

When Mary Delany visited Castle Ward in 1762 she was so moved she remarked: 'altogether one of the finest places I ever saw'. Many modern visitors will share this opinion, for the 800-acre landscape park at Castle Ward, overlooking an inlet of Strangford Lough, remains a place of idyllic and serene beauty. For the garden historian, it is also a place of considerable interest as the park has residual remains of a history of garden development spanning four centuries.

Visitors to the grounds should park their car in the farmyard close to the tower house built by the Ward family in the late sixteenth century. From here there is a path into the park where a short distance north west, on a slight ascent, stands the site of a grand house built by the Wards around 1710. This was demolished in the mid nineteenth century, but much survives of its surrounding formal gardens laid out in the 1720s. These include splendid yew terraces forming two tunnels sixty-metres long, the site of a canal between two recently replanted double rows of limes, and a 530-metre long canal known as the Temple Water – the largest ornamental garden feature to survive in Ireland from the early eighteenth century. The scale and grandeur of this feature is particularly impressive when viewed from the south-west end where it is aligned upon the much earlier Audley's Castle. The adjacent early nineteenth-century Walled Garden now houses a wildfowl collection, while on the slopes above the charming Lady Anne's Temple, built around 1750, commands the scene. From here the visitor will view the Temple Water as well as the surrounding informal landscape park – laid out between 1758 and 1767 as a setting for the present house some distance to the south.

In the mid nineteenth century the park was enlarged and a major reorganisation of the gardens took place around the house. On the site of the old Georgian flower garden the Wards built the terraced Windsor Garden. Its sunken area, which once held an elaborate parterre, now has a small circular pond with a statue of Neptune, but the bedding arrangement on the terraces largely retains its Victorian layout while the symmetrically placed cordylines and the screen of Irish yews on the west side perpetuate the formal planting design. The adjacent Pinetum, also established around 1840, contains a collection of spruces, pines, firs and other trees introduced from America and the Pacific in

Victorian times. A large rockery built against the wall of the old garden is an Edwardian addition to the garden.

The house and demesne are now splendidly maintained by the National Trust.

Located 1 mile west of Strangford on the Downpatrick Road. NGR: J 573494. Open daily from dawn to dusk. Castle Ward house open from April to October (days and times may vary). Restaurant and gift shop in stable-yard open as house. Toilet facilities. Mostly suitable for wheelchairs. Dogs on lead. Admission: £3.00 per car and £1.50 when house and other facilities are closed (entrance to house extra). Tel: (039686) 204.

Lady Anne's Temple, Castle Ward

CASTLEWELLAN NATIONAL ARBORETUM

County Down

Irish gardens, for the most part, make their impact with trees. They provide the essential elements of overall design and give diversity at all scales and in all seasons. The mild and moist climate of Ireland is also remarkably favourable to their growth and undoubtedly there is no better place to appreciate this than in the National Arboretum at Castlewellan – home of an outstanding collection of mature trees and shrubs.

The arboretum was established by the fifth Earl of Annesley (1831–1909) who inherited Castlewellan demesne from his brother in 1874. This lush allotment was originally confined to the Walled Garden area, a short distance north east of a huge baronial castle that had been built between 1856 and 1859 with glorious prospects of the park and the Mourne Mountains. In 1967 the demesne together with the arboretum were purchased from the late Gerald Annesley by the Forest Service and two years later opened as a Forest Park. The arboretum, which originally covered no more than fifteen acres, has since been considerably expanded and now covers more than one hundred.

The hub of the collection is the Walled Garden, now called the Annesley Garden. It is divided by a wall into two portions: the Upper Garden, originally built in 1740 to cultivate kitchen produce, and to the south east the larger Lower Garden – laid out in the 1850s as a pleasure ground with terraces, a fountain and ornamental trees. The two areas are united by a formal axis running down through the centre, which in the Upper Garden is lined with herbaceous borders backed with clipped yew hedges.

The main entrance brings the visitor into the Lower Garden, passing the old gardener's house on the left. The path here has some striking Chilean fire-bushes (*Embothrium coccineum* 'Longifolium'), rhododendrons and maples. The path to the right passes a large *Chamaecyparis pisifera* 'Squarrosa' first introduced from Japan in 1862 and now a popular cultivar. As in many old arboreta, the family *Chamaecyparis* is well represented and there are over forty varieties here. Further down the path and flanking a flight of steps stand the oldest trees in the garden – a pair of Wellingtonia (*Sequoiadendron giganteum*) planted in 1856 no less than three years after the species was first introduced from Sierra Nevada. Close by an extremely large Monterey cypress, *Cupressus macrocarpa* 'Lutea', is hard to miss; this is the mother tree of *Cupressus* x *Cupressocyparis leylandii* 'Castlewellan Gold', one of the best-known but perhaps least endearing trees in this arboretum. It was discovered in 1962 by the then head gardener John Keown after extracting and sowing seeds from a cone-laden branch. Millions of these trees now grace (or disgrace) the gardens of the world, not least in Ireland where they are commonly associated with brash bungalows.

In the same area along this path stands a slow-growing *Cordyline indivisa* 'Vera' – one of a large number of notable plants at Castlewellan that comes from New Zealand. Amongst others is the genus *Podocarpus* of which there are fifteen species; visitors will also discover good specimens of the evergreen *Carpodetus serratus*, the aromatic *Pseudowintera colorata*, the unusual kawaka (*Libocedrus plumosa*) and an exceptionally beautiful *Pseudopanax laetus*.

Many fine trees grace the area around the heron fountain where the planting becomes even more profuse – here, for example, a large specimen of *Picea smithiana*, planted in 1868 and now seventy-five-feet tall, makes its home. There are forty-two members of this genus in the arboretum. Close by stands a lovely *Myrtus apiculata* and, also from Chile, a remarkable *Pilgerodendron uviferum*. Throughout the arboretum there are generally some thirty species, varieties and cultivars of the Juniper genus, including a *Juniperus recurva* that is fifty-feet tall. The silver fir is also well represented with forty-five members, the oldest an Algerian fir, *Abies numidica*, planted in 1886. Among the most dignified plants from the southern hemisphere is a fine Tasmanian waratah, *Telopea truncata*, while along the north-east wall leading up to the greenhouses stretches a magnificent avenue of late summer-flowering eucryphia.

The Edwardian greenhouses in the corner of the Lower Garden contain quite a variety of fuchsia, passiflora and tibouchina, as well as specimens of *Lapageria rosea* and *Wattakaka sinensis*. Like jewels in a box, one greenhouse encases a small collection of free-flying tropical birds; in the two adjacent end houses lush collections of ferns and phormiums grow.

Immediately north of the Annesley Garden lies an extensive collection of spring-flowering trees, mainly prunus and malus planted between 1972 and 1974. A prodiguous grouping of dwarf conifers also thrives here; sown in 1976, the trees occupy four long, curved beds. In the shade of the beech trees to the north is a five-acre rhododendron garden which also includes camellias and large numbers of deciduous azaleas. Two duck ponds on the fringe of this area display many outstanding trees within their vicinity, including a very tall red silver fir (*Abies amabilis*).

Aside from the main arboretum, Castlewellan offers much more to the intrepid visitor. Bring sturdy boots for long walks around the lough, through the woods and up the mountain ridge. Wonderful.

Located in Castlewellan, 4 miles north west of Newcastle. NGR: J 335371. Open daily from dawn to dusk. Refreshments available during summer months. Toilet facilities. Partly suitable for wheelchairs. Dogs on lead. Admission: £2.20 per car. Tel: (03967) 78664.

MOUNT STEWART

County Down

Great gardens are often the achievement of one outstanding creator and none more so than at Mount Stewart. When Edith, Marchioness of Londonderry, first arrived at Mount Stewart in 1921 she found a dank and gloomy scene around the late Georgian classical house and immediately determined to effect a complete transformation. She succeeded and created a distinctive formal and informal garden with an incomparable plant collection whose youth is disguised by the exceptionally high humidity from the sea.

Lady Londonderry's work on the gardens was aided by the ample labour force available after the Great War, while much advice was forthcoming from such eminent gardeners as Sir John Ross and Gertrude Jekyll. The staggering range of plants she used came from nurseries throughout the Empire, while she corresponded with plant collectors Clarance Elliott, George Forrest and Frank Kingdon Ward. Her approach was to try to grow as many rare and tender plants as possible, especially those giving a tropical effect. Ultimately her woody plant collection was dominated by southern-hemisphere species, with the Australian taxa remaining the most important. On her death in 1959, she left behind a garden of seventy-eight acres comprising formal garden areas, terracing, pergolas, pavilions, woodland gardens and a water garden encircling a large lake in the park. Today it is generally acknowledged as one of the greatest gardens in western Europe and is maintained in splendid order by the National Trust who assumed control of the property in 1955. Indeed over the past twenty years under the present head gardener Nigel Marshall, direct seed acquisition from America and Australia has again become an important feature of this garden.

Undoubtedly the most important genus at Mount Stewart is the eucalyptus. Today there are no less than eighty plants of fifteen taxa in the garden – the oldest a mammoth specimen of *E. globulus* planted in 1894 on the Fountain Walk close to the car park. This species grows especially well at Mount Stewart, with some reaching a height of 120 feet. Indeed this garden probably has the most concentrated planting of *E. globulus* in northern Europe and everywhere their resinous scent fills the air.

Close to the Fountain Walk lies the Mairi Garden, a white-and-blue creation laid out in 1925. Beside the

Mount Stewart's formal Italian garden

summer house overlooking this small garden is an enormous *Cordyline australis*, one of a number here. *Cordyline* is a speciality at Mount Stewart, with five taxa cultivated, and there are some exceptionally fine specimens of *C. indivisa*. Another important genus at Mount Stewart, *Olearia*, thrives here – notably groups of the larger type *O. paniculata* with their undulating foliage.

From the Mairi Garden a path leads up to the Dodo Terrace, built in 1925 and decorated with a range of amusing stone ornaments made by Thomas Beattie, a local craftsman, to Lady Londonderry's designs. This overlooks the Italian Garden – a large rectangular area below the south front of the house divided by a wide grassy verge into two identical parterres, the design of which was based on the south-western parterre at Dunrobin Castle, the home of Lady Londonderry's mother. The beds are edged with purple berberis and golden thuja and have a colour scheme ranging from grey-white and blue in the west to orange and scarlet in the east. Below this area visitors will discern a tall specimen of *Chamaerops humilis*, a fine example of the primitive New Zealand tree *Phyllocladus glaucus*, and a magnificent specimen of *Sophora tetraptera*, undoubtedly New Zealand's most beautiful tree.

A flight of wide, curving steps leads down to a smaller garden with an oval pond and Spanish-style loggia on axis with the house. Arches of Monterey cypress enclose the area on three sides, contributing to a feeling of seclusion. Behind the arches on the west side lies the Peace Garden and beyond this the Lily Wood – an area of light woodland with many rare trees and shrubs. The Chilean myrtle, *Myrtus apiculata*, grows to huge sizes here and naturally regenerates in thickets.

On the west side of the house the Sunken Garden has been laid out based on a plan sent to Lady Londonderry by Gertrude Jekyll in 1920. It is surrounded on three sides by a pergola with roses, vine, clematis species and the rare *Billardiera longiflora*, with its blue autumnal berries. Beds flanking a central lawn, delimited with scalloped hedges of sweet bay, have brilliant orange azaleas in spring and a rich mixture of herbaceous plants in summer. Among the surviving early plants of this garden is an unusual *Hakea lissosperma* whose acicular leaves and form match the *Erica arborea*.

The paved Shamrock Garden immediately to the west is enclosed by a high hedge of *Cupressus macro-*

Lakeside planting at Mount Stewart

carpa surmounted by scenes of a hunt taken from Queen Mary's Psalter in the British Library. More topiary here includes shapes of an Irish harp and a bear formed of yew and a fine *Acer palmatum* 'Senkaki' positioned at a focal point. The charm of this garden is somewhat spoiled by a vulgar bed shaped as the Red Hand of Ulster.

In the adjacent Memorial Glade planted in 1960 an avenue of *Embothrium coccineum* stretches out – a much-used plant at Mount Stewart. The path northwards to the lake brings the visitor past a number of pittosporum varieties, another speciality of this garden, notably a specimen of *P. bicolor*. Along the west side of the lake are vigorous growths of *Weinmannia trichosperma* from Chile and nearby is an attractively barked *Betula albo-sinensis septentrionalis* from China. The lake, originally dug in 1840, was landscaped by Lady Londonderry – following Jekyll's advice its margins were planted with silver-stemmed birches. For autumn colour she added masses of maples and the attractive *Cercidiphyllum japonicum*, while groups of *Salix alba* 'Sericea' and 'Vitellina' provide bright colour in winter.

On the hill north of the lake lies 'Tir nan Og' – the private burial ground of the Stewart family. The slopes around this hill contain many rare and tender plants, including a number of *Callitris oblonga*, two fine specimens of the flamboyant *Metrosideros lucida*, a tall *Myrtus obcordata*, a fine *Cupressus cashmeriana*, and a very rare *Malus kansuensis*, probably one of the few Wilson-collected plants at Mount Stewart. The route back to the house along the Jubilee Avenue with its statue of a white stag and down the Ladies Walk brings the visitor past many attractive rhododendrons flourishing in the shadow of the fir *Pseudotsuga menziesii*. Before leaving, visitors should walk down to the Temple of the Winds (circa 1785, architect James Stuart), a private dining-house magnificently sited overlooking Strangford Lough – Ulster's finest garden building.

Located 5 miles south east of Newtownards at Greyabbey on the Portaferry Road (A20). NGR: J 552698. Open daily, April to August: 10.30 am – 6.00 pm. September and October: weekends only, 12.00 – 6.00 pm. House open April to October. Refreshments open as house. Gift shop. Toilet facilities. Partly suitable for wheelchairs. Dogs on lead. Admission: adults £2.70; children £1.35 (entrance to house extra). Tel: (024774) 387.

ROWALLANE

County Down

Centre walk in the walled garden at Rowallane

There are few gardens anywhere in the British Isles that so successfully combine the artistic with the practical in such complete accord with their site as Rowallane. The impressive range of plants in this fifty-acre garden, notably its rhododendrons for which it is famous, have been skilfully grouped in the handsomely undulating site to create a charming, uncluttered effect that is as much a joy to the plantsman as to the artist. Although normally associated with spectacular spring-colour displays, Rowallane also has an extensive collection of summer-flowering plants, especially in the Walled Garden, while additional interest is provided by a large rock garden, a fine collection of trees and wildflower meadows.

The groundwork of the garden was laid down by Reverend John Moore following the completion of the house in 1861. It involved reclaiming a barren hillside of rock and gorse and creating a series of plantations, a walled garden and an extensive pleasure ground. Reverend Moore died in 1903 and bequeathed the property to his nephew, Hugh Armytage Moore, who was the man responsible for creating the gardens as we know them today. With his rare gift for planning and great eye for plants, he developed Rowallane using many of the novel plants of his day. Armytage Moore had close contacts with the Edinburgh Botanic Gardens among other places and raised many of his plants from seed collected by the great plant hunters of the early twentieth century, such as Wilson, Forrest and Kingdon Ward. He also developed a number of his own hybrids and was awarded the Victoria Medal of Honour by the Royal Horticultural Society in 1942 for his work. In 1955 the National Trust took over the running of his gardens, which are still maintained much as they were in Armytage Moore's time. The house is now the headquarters of the National Trust in Northern Ireland.

The avenue leading up to the house passes through much fine woodland, with arboreal rhododendrons and mossy rocks on either side and a series of idiosyncratic stone seats, cairns and ornaments built by Reverend Moore in the nineteenth century. From the car park visitors walk up to the house, passing the Home Wood where there are mainly large-leafed, late-flowering rhododendrons sheltered below beech and Scots pine. Species to delight in here include the yellow-flowering *Rhododendron macabeanum*, *R. basilicum* and the glabrous evergreen *Trochodendron aralioides*.

The Walled Garden beside the house contains a splendid collection of flowering herbaceous plants and some excellent shrub roses. Along the north side grow great clumps of *Meconopsis*, including the most popular Himyalayan blue poppy *M. grandis* and a local variety, *M. x sheldonii* 'Slieve Donard'. In midsummer the various primulas put on a great display, especially the vigorous natural hybrid *Primula* 'Rowallane Rose' which seeded itself here in the days of Armytage Moore. Early-flowering shrubs in the area include magnolias, *Vibernum plicatum tomentosum* 'Rowallane' and many other tender subjects. The national collection of large-flowered penstemons is held at Rowallane and makes an excellent end-of-season show. Varieties to note include 'Garnet', 'Burgandy' and 'Sour Grapes', with delicious shades of crimson. Also eager to impress are a group of showy gloxina-like varieties characterised by clear white-throated flowers in reds and crimson.

The outer Walled Garden, formerly a nursery area, provides shelter for a variety of hostas and a collection of hydrangeas, notably the large *H. sargentiana*. Visitors will find the original *Chaenomeles* x *superba* 'Rowallane' here, as well as the famous *Hypericum* 'Rowallane' hybrid which began as a seedling self-sown in the Rock Garden. It has a large yellow cup and glossy green foliage and is considered the most beautiful St John's wort in cultivation.

Passing through the Haggard area where the bursting seed capsules of a *Populus maximowiczii* resemble snow in July and August, the visitor arrives in the Spring Ground – a series of undulating slopes whose banks are covered with beds of azaleas and rhododendrons. Wildflowers are encouraged and the area has a high content of devilsbit scabious producing a beautiful blue haze in summer. During autumn there is much

Rhododendron chilsenii *in walled garden, Rowallane*

colour from maples and azaleas and tints of *Prunus sargentii*.

North east a narrow valley called the Stream Ground, which G. Forrest once styled as 'a bit of Yunnan', curves downward. It contains many triflorum rhododendrons as well as a boggy pool with royal ferns and bog arums. Beyond stretches the Hospital where visitors will come across a fine handkerchief tree, *Davidia involucrata*, and an immense *Desfontainea spinosa*. South east through the Old Wood lies the recently restored Rock Garden – a vast upheaval of natural whinstone accommodating a wide range of alpines, heathers and dwarf rhododendrons. More

Azaleas in spring ground, Rowallane

dwarf rhododendrons surround the Bishop's Rock, while further to the west the New Ground produces large rhododendrons and a number of fine trees, including a magnificent *Chamaecyparis nootkatensis*. Beyond lies Trio Hill with its brilliant orange red-flowering *Embothrium coccineum*. Among the many conifers here are fine specimens of *Cupressus lusitanica* 'Glauca Pendula' and *Tsuga yunnanensis*. Back across the Spring Ground the visitor should inspect the Paddock with its fine species of *Sorbus* and magnificent southern beeches before returning to the stable-yard.

The Pleasure Grounds – a lovely parkland that extends behind the house – are well worth a visit before leaving. Many of the fine trees here were planted by Reverend Moore in the last century and include *Tsuga mertensiana* and *Glyptostrobus pensilis*. Wildflowers are profuse here and grow in abundance; the variety of orchids is truly glorious: twayblade, greater butterfly and species of *Dactylorrhiza*. It's a butterfly paradise.

Located ½ mile south of Saintfield on the Downpatrick Road (A7). NGR: J 109576. Open weekdays in March: 10.30 am – 5.00 pm. April to October: weekdays, 10.30 am – 6. 00 pm; weekends, 2. 00 – 6. 00 pm. November to March: weekdays, 9.00 am – 5.00 pm. Closed 25, 26 December and 1 January. Tea rooms with light refreshments open April to September: 2.00 – 6.00 pm. Gift shop. Toilet facilities. Partly suitable for wheelchairs. Dogs on lead. Admission: £2.50 (March to October); £1.90 (November to February). Tel: (0238) 510131.

SEAFORDE

County Down

In recent years a particularly worthwhile horticultural development has been the placing of nurseries beside gardens open to the public. In this way plants admired and seen flourishing in the garden may be purchased next door. This is well illustrated at Seaforde where, in addition to a garden and nursery, there is also a butterfly house.

The Seaforde garden occupies the southern half of a five-acre walled garden on the perimeter of a beautiful demesne park, probably created by the great eighteenth-century landscape designer John Sutherland. Visitors arrive by the Downpatrick gate on the Belfast Road and drive through pleasant woodland to a car park, formerly the estate tree nursery. From here the garden is approached through the northern part of the Walled Garden, once devoted to kitchen produce and now the site of a large commercial nursery with a fine choice of trees and shrubs for sale.

The garden one sees today was created in the 1970s by the present owners, Patrick and Lady Anthea Forde, on the site of a formal Victorian ornamental flower garden. Entering through a gate from the north-west end, the visitor should turn left along the wall where there are some attractive plants, notably a good selection of echiums, on the site of the old greenhouses and camellia house. Further along is a recently built Mogul-style tower with a spiral staircase, a small herb garden and a Gothic arbour, while south of this lies a large hornbeam maze constructed in 1975. Its entrance is delimited by two stone urns re-used from the old Victorian garden; those managing to reach the centre will find an arbour with a statue of Diana. Flanking the maze and across lawns are two avenues of shrubs containing the national collection of eucryphias. At present nineteen cultivars of these fragrant, white-flowering southern-hemisphere shrubs blossom at Seaforde, including new types with variegated leaves recently found in Tasmania.

On the south side of the Walled Garden the Pheasantry emerges: a secluded, undulating grassy area with specimen trees and shrubs. Of special note is an enormous *Rhododendron arboreum* and a magnificent Crimean pine (*Pinus nigra caramanica*). A small pond has *Gunnera manicata* on its banks, while at least eleven varieties of azaras have been planted in the shade of the trees on the south-east side.

Those interested in tropical plants should find it edifying to visit the Butterfly House on the west side of the nursery. Built in 1988 and now quite a popular attraction, it contains a good selection of tree ferns, including no less than three varieties of *Dicksonia* and *Cyathea*. Some of the attractive tropical planting features the African *Cyperus papyrus*, the banana plant *Musa basjoo*, the violet-flowering *Lantana camara* and the Brazilian spider-flower *Tibouchina semidecandra*. Also from Brazil is a jacaranda with downy, fern-like leaves, while from South Africa are varieties of plumbago and from Japan varieties of nerium and philodendron. Among the datura shrubs is the striking *D. suaveolens* from Mexico with its large, pendulous, trumpet-shaped fragrant white flowers.

Located just north of Seaforde on the Ballynahinch Road. NGR: J 403433. Open daily, Easter to October: weekdays and Saturdays, 10.00 am – 5.00 pm; Sundays, 2.00 – 6.00 pm. Nursery and Butterfly House open all year round. Refreshments available. Toilet facilities. Suitable for wheelchairs. No dogs. Admission to garden: adults £2.00; senior citizens and children £1.20. Admission to Butterfly House: adults £2.00; senior citizens and children £1.20. Tel: (039687) 225.

FERNHILL

County Dublin

Fernhill is a garden where the plants come first, not the architecture. Covering some forty acres in a superb location overlooking Dublin Bay, it contains a comprehensive collection of trees and shrubs in an informal 'Robinsonian' layout that adapts the plants to the terrain. The camellias, magnolias and rhododendrons are particularly fine, as are the large drifts of spring bulbs, but there is something for everyone amongst the many excellent plants that thrive in the light woodlands, water garden, rockery, heather bank, fernery and kitchen garden of this enchanted place.

Although there are some fine eighteenth-century trees at Fernhill, the structure of the present garden layout was created in the 1860s by Mr Justice Darley and his son Edmond. It was further enlarged in the 1890s by Judge William Darley who was responsible for the pond, cascades, rockery and for many of the fine rhododendrons, including a magnificent bright blue form of *R. augustinii* and the original plant of the pink-flowering *R.* 'Fernhill Silver' – an arboreum hybrid of unknown origin but believed to have been given to Fernhill by the Glasnevin Botanic Gardens. The rhododendron collection was expanded by Joseph Walker after he acquired the property in 1934, and his work improving and extending the garden was subsequently continued by Ralph and Susan Walker when they succeeded to Fernhill in the 1940s. In addition to adding new features such as the Back Paddock, Water Garden and Heather Bank, they increased the collections enormously and transformed the garden by putting into practice William Robinson's ideas of arranging exotic plants in a naturalistic setting.

Visitors start and finish their tour at the bottom end of this long, narrow garden opposite the nursery sales area. The Kitchen Garden, which is located some distance downslope from the house, is the first area to be visited. It is enclosed within clipped beech hedges and is divided into four quadrants with a now rarely seen *potager*-style layout that was once a standard feature of most Irish walled gardens. Typically, herbaceous borders line the paths with espalier apple trees behind screening rows of vegetables and soft fruit. There is also a small Edwardian rose garden with clipped box hedges delimiting beds of floribunda roses and old hybrid teas. Among the latter are a number of early Dickson-bred varieties, such as 'Irish Elegance', bred in 1903, with a lovely shade of salmon pink.

A large beech tree spreads over the avenue up to the house, beyond which stands a fine sweet chestnut at least 200-years old. Great masses of colchicums blossom beneath this tree in autumn, while in spring thousands of daffodils, mostly old unnamed varieties, flower along the avenue, on the lawns and in the sloping field in front of the house.

A long straight track known as the Broadwalk brings the visitor from the open areas around the house into a lovely light woodland full of beeches, oak and larches. Three splendid Wellingtonias 130-feet high date from the time the Broadwalk was laid out and were planted in the 1860s, while other impressive trees along here include a *Tsuga heterophylla* seventy-nine-feet high and further down, a Scots pine 108-feet tall. Enthusiasts will admire two more trees: a good *Cedrus deodara* and a *Dacrydium cupressinum*, but it is the shrubs, particularly the rhododendrons, that are the glory of these woods. Aside from the older *R. arboreum* varieties, the area has a large number of fine species, including examples of *R. genestierianum*, a Forrest introduction from Burma; *R. macabeanum* with magnificent trusses of pale yellow, purple-blotched flowers; a magnificent *R. falconeris* with rust-coloured tomentum on the underside of its large obovate leaves; and a tender white-flowering *R. lindleyi*. The sloping stony ground is ideal for these plants, especially in the area of the old quarry to the right of the Broadwalk where they grow as if they were in the Himalayas. Among the many other praiseworthy plants is a well-developed *Michelia doltsopa* from China – a rare relation of the magnolia with creamy-white flowers.

In complete contrast to the wild character of this part of the woodland is the laurel lawn off the Broadwalk – a rarely seen surviver from the Victorian days and kept in immaculate condition. At the very end of the Broadwalk lies the Back Paddock, a new addition to the garden laid down by Ralph Walker in 1952 and containing many fine shrubs, notably varieties of camellia, leptospermum and pieris. Taking the quarry path from here, the visitor will pass the Fernery, arrive back onto the Broadwalk and then take the path around the house past the tennis court area with its attractive tulip tree. The principal attraction along this route is an old Edwardian rockery which the Walkers cleared, enlarged and planted with an amazing mixture of pieris, cordylines, bulbs, perennials, rhododendrons, azaleas, as well as a variety of alpines. Of note is the

Rhododendron 'Bric-a-Brac' (a hybrid between *R. moupinense* and *R. leucaspis*) whose beautiful little flowers are among the first to open each year in the garden. The Walkers also added a heather bank to the side of the Rockery and amongst the erica that grow here are varieties of bergenia, most notably *Bergenia* 'Ballawley' – one of few surviving cultivars from the late Desmond Shaw-Smith's vanished nursery at Ballawley Park nearby.

A hillside stream behind the house was widened and dammed by the Walkers to create waterfalls and little pools for a water garden. This garden now contains a variety of waterside plants, such as the yellow skunk cabbage *Lysichiton americanus*, rodgersias and astilbes, while on the banks above verdant plantings of ferns, pulmonarias and many candelabra members of the primula genus flourish. Nearby lies Mrs Walker's famed collection of primulas which no visitor to Fernhill should miss before leaving the garden.

Located 8 miles south of central Dublin in Sandyford on the Enniskerry Road. NGR: O 183257. Open daily, March to November: Tuesdays to Saturdays and bank holidays, 11.00 am – 5.00 pm; Sundays, 2.00 – 6.00 pm. Plant nursery. Occasional exhibitions of sculpture. Toilet facilities. Partly suitable for wheelchairs. No dogs. Admission: adults IR £2.50; senior citizens and students IR £1.50; children IR £1.00 (children under 5 free). Special adult group rates (20 +) IR £2.00 each. Tel: (01) 2956000.

MALAHIDE CASTLE GARDENS

County Dublin

Most Irish gardens rely on ericaceous plants such as rhododendrons to provide their main displays of colour, but at Malahide these are largely precluded by the alkalinity of the soil (around pH 7). Prominence has thus been given to the many lime-tolerant genera so often bypassed in favour of more eye-catching plants. The scent from philadelphus, syringa, deutzia and old roses more than compensates for any lack of colour, while the enormous range of non-ericaceous plants at Malahide – one of the most impressive of its kind in these islands – is particularly admired for its collections of ceanothus, clematis, crocosmia, eryngium, escallonia, euphorbia, hebe, hypericum, olearia and pittosporum.

The gardens cover twenty acres, including a four-acre walled garden, and lie to the west and north of Malahide Castle. They form part of a 250-acre demesne park acquired by Dublin County Council in 1976 following the death of Lord Talbot de Malahide. The history of the Talbots at Malahide stretches back to the end of the twelfth century, but the gardens are the creation of Milo, the seventh Lord Talbot de Malahide – a noted plantsman who assembled a collection of over 5,000 species and cultivars between 1948 and 1973. Close connections with Australia resulted in Australasian genera being particularly well represented, but Lord Talbot also had a fondness for South American plants and was a recognised authority on the genus *Olearia* – interests that are still reflected in the planting today.

Visitors approach the main garden – a varied mixture of trees and shrubs known as the West Lawn – from the front of the castle. Passing just beyond a blue conifer, *Cupressus glabra* 'Pyramidalis', the main focus of the garden layout comes into view on the left – a spacious lawn dominated by a large cedar with spreading cyclamen below. The main shrubberies, divided by a network of grass rides and interlinking paths, are to the right, while the avenue area, which also contains some rare and outstanding plants, lies on the opposite side of the lawn.

The shrubberies are entered by a long tarmacadam path flanked by borders containing a variety of shrubs and herbaceous perennials, many noted for their fragrance as well as for their flowers. Among these are the Californian poppy (*Romneya coulteri*), the large white-flowering *Philadelphus* 'Beauclerk', the honey-scented yellow *Pittosporum eugenioides* 'Variegatum', and the flowering quince *Chaenomeles speciosa* 'Vermillion'. Here also lies a large-leaved *Meliosma dillineifolia*, while off the grass rides to the north east stand several interesting trees, including an unusual variety of the strawberry tree (*Arbutus unedo* 'Rubra'), a very large wide-spreading *Pterocarya fraxinifolia* and the rarely seen *Aralia spinosa*, known as the devil's walking stick because of its viciously spiny stems.

The path around the lawn in front of the castle brings the visitor past some fine shrubs and specimen trees, most notably the aromatic *Ozothamnus ledifolius* from Tasmania, the Mexican orange blossom (*Choisya ternata*) and the Mount Etna broom (*Genista aetnensis*) which in midsummer yields a profusion of fragrant pea-like golden-yellow flowers. From here the visitor passes through the old main avenue area where a number of different species of olearias and hydrangeas flower, in addition to podocarpus shrubs, crinodendrons, magnolias and even a tender hakea in the shade of the trees. The return path, past a hedge of *Cotoneaster conspicuus* and some fine sorbus trees, leads the visitor to the south-west wall of the castle with its magnificent *Magnolia grandiflora* whose large creamy-white fragrant flowers continue to bloom throughout the summer. More plants are found behind the castle, including some old roses and the spectacular vine *Vitis coignetiae*.

The finest part of the Malahide plant collection lies in the four-acre Walled Garden, but problems with vandals in recent years have meant that this part of the garden is only open on Wednesday afternoons. The area is subdivided into several sections, each with an identity of its own. The first of these, the old Rose Garden, is used for testing the hardiness of new tender species as they become available, while the section beyond, known as the Haggard, has a selection of cottage-type plants as well as a number of wall plants and climbers. One of the two glasshouses here shelters a small collection of tender species, including *Luculia gratissima* 'Rosea' and the bromeliad *Puya alpestris*. A small enclosed yard beyond the Haggard reveals raised beds of alpine plants as well as shrubs – notably *Banksia dentata*, *Acradenia frankliniae* and *Eucryphia milliganii*. As this yard is so small, the area formerly known as the Tresco Wall has been altered to

Daffodils in Malahide Castle Gardens

accommodate a large collection of alpines.

From the new alpine beds and the reconstructed sunken greenhouse, the garden opens out onto a wide lawn of shrubberies. Among the plants here are a number of garryas raised from seed by Lord Talbot. It was from this selection that he chose the hybrid which won him an Award of Merit from the Royal Horticultural Society, later named *Garrya* x *issaquahensis* 'Pat Ballard'. There are two greenhouses here, one of which contains the rare *Paeonia cambessedesii*, while to the south a large pond succours *Gunnera manicata* along its banks. An old peach house containing a selection of tender climbing plants and correa species lies along the south wall in addition to a shrubbery full of exotic plants: *Clematis* 'Etoile Rose', *Azara dentata*, the silk tree *Albizia julibrissin* 'Rosea' and the vigorous yellow-flowering *Fremontodendron* 'California Glory'.

Located in Malahide, 9 miles north of Dublin. NGR: O 220452. Open daily, May to October: 2.00 – 5.00 pm. Guided tours available every Wednesday at 2.00 pm (including Walled Garden and the castle). The Walled Garden is open to groups by special appointment. Lunches and teas available in the castle. Gift shop. Toilet facilities. Suitable for wheelchairs. Dogs on lead. Admission: adults IR £1.00; senior citizens and children free. Tel: (01) 8450940.

NATIONAL BOTANIC GARDENS, GLASNEVIN

County Dublin

Although the principal object of botanic gardens is to maintain collections of plant species for the purpose of study, many can be pleasant and instructive places to visit. The National Botanic Gardens at Glasnevin, Ireland's premier botanical and horticultural establishment, is a rewarding and attractive garden for gardeners and non-gardeners alike. Occupying a beautiful forty-eight acre site on the banks of the Tolka River, it contains over 20,000 different plant species and cultivars including many exceptional specimens. There are some lovely trees, many outstanding displays of shrubs and perennials and, of course, the famous glasshouses, including Turner's magnificent curvilinear range.

The botanic gardens were established in 1795 under the auspices of the Dublin Society, later the Royal Dublin Society, at the behest of the Irish Parliament to 'promote a scientific knowledge in the various branches of agriculture'. The twenty-seven-acre site chosen for the garden lay outside the hamlet of Glasnevin on the former demesne of Thomas Tickell, a minor poet and ardent admirer of Joseph Addison, the statesman and writer. A survival from this period is a double line of yew trees known as Addison's Walk which Tickell probably planted in memory of his much esteemed patron. The original botanic gardens were laid out by their first director, Dr Walter Wade, Professor of Botany to the Dublin Society, with the help of the first superintendent, John Underwood. After Wade's death in 1825 the gardens went into a period of decline but were resurrected and redesigned by the new director Ninian Nivan between 1834 and 1838, with further modifications carried out by his successors Dr David Moore (1838–79), Sir Frederick Moore (1879–1922), J. W. Besant (1922–44) and Dr T. J. Walsh (1944–68).

Over the past two centuries the gardens have played a central role in botanical and horticultural advancement in Ireland. Plants and seeds have been imported and new cultivars and species distributed to gardeners and nurserymen. The fastigate gorse *Ulex europaeus* 'Strictus', found at Mount Stewart in 1804, was the first cultivar to be introduced from Glasnevin and this has been followed by numerous others, such as the pampas grass *Cortaderia selloana*, the pink-flushed lily *Crinum moorei* from Nepal, the beautiful Chatham

Island daisy-bush (*Olearia semidentata*), the exquisitely scented *Abelia triflora*, and the giant lily *Cardiocrinum giganteum*. In the 1840s orchids were cultivated from seed to flowering stage for the first time at Glasnevin and it was here in 1869 that hybridisation of the insectivorous pitcher-plants sarracenia was first carried out successfully.

The soil of the Glasnevin Botanic Gardens is heavy alkaline boulder clay, which confines the growing of calcifuge plants such as rhododendrons and ericas to specially prepared peat beds. There are, however, a wide range of habitats within the garden and these are incorporated within a botanical rather than geographical layout. They include special areas devoted to roses, ground cover plants, economic and poisonous plants, native plants and herbs and vegetables. Glasnevin also houses a large rockery, a bog garden, a wild garden and a double, curving herbaceous border which is a marvellous sight in summer.

Many more plants are grown in the Victorian glasshouses. These buildings have long been a great attraction of Glasnevin, especially the curvilinear range which was commissioned by David Moore in the 1840s and is now in the process of being restored. The central pavilion and one wing of this range was built by Richard Turner, the Dublin-born ironmaster, and completed in 1848. Twenty years later Turner ingeniously doubled the building in size by removing the walls and extending it back. The Great Palm House containing the tropical tree collection and notable now for its cycads was built in 1884, while its side wings, housing orchids and flowering pot plants, belong to an earlier building. On the east side of the garden lies the Victoria or Aquatic House which was built in 1854 to protect the gigantic Amazon water lily – at that time only recently introduced and one of the wonders of the age. The lily can still be seen growing here during the summer months. On one side of this building lies the Cactus and Succulent House built in 1890, while on the other stands the Fern House – a rather dull aluminium glasshouse constructed in 1966 to replace an attractive Victorian octagonal conservatory. This Fern House is divided into separate compartments for tree ferns and tropical species. Here amidst dense foliage the visitor will find the native but rare Killarney fern *Trichomanes speciosum* and the Australian tree fern *Todea barbara*, which had been transferred here in 1969 from the old Trinity College Botanic Gardens and is reputed to be 400-years old.

Although the gardens at Glasnevin will celebrate their bicentenary in 1995, very few of the trees and shrubs were planted more than a century ago. One of the older plants is the Chusan palm (*Trachycarpus fortunei*), planted outside the curvilinear range in 1870. Other majestic, patriarchal trees are a *Cedrus atlantantica* 'Pendula' planted some time before 1877 and a large *Zelkova carpinifolia* that looks especially good in winter. A remarkable early Victorian chain tent draped with a venerable wisteria is not to be missed – years ago it had a weeping ash growing in the centre but this has long since been replaced with a steel pole. One of the most popular sights in the garden, however, is 'The last Rose of Summer' – a cultivar of the China rose *R. chinensis* 'Old Blush'. It was raised from a cutting taken from a rose at Jenkinstown House in County Kilkenny which, according to tradition, was the rose that inspired Thomas Moore to write his famous ballad.

Located 1 mile north of Dublin in Glasnevin. NGR: O 152373. Open daily, except 25 December: summer, 9.00 am – 6.00 pm; winter, 9.00 am – 4.30 pm. Parking on road outside of gates. Gift shop. Toilet facilities. Suitable for wheelchairs (except Palm House). Dogs on lead. Admission: free. Tel: (01) 374388.

FLORENCE COURT

County Fermanagh

There is something dream-like about Florence Court
whose golden-grey façade, with its almost timeless,
bucolic quality, glistens like a jewel amidst the splen-
dour of superb parkland and majestic mountain
scenery. In addition to its attractive late eighteenth-
century landscape park, Florence Court also has a
Victorian pleasure ground, a walled garden and, above
all, the mother of all Irish yews: *Taxus baccata*
'Fastigiata'.

The five-acre Walled Garden in the woods to the
north of the house is best visited first. It is divided into
two portions by a brick wall and delimited along its
east and south sides by two long ornamental ponds.
Like most Irish walled gardens, it once had a *potager*
layout with a mixture of vegetables, flowers and fruit
trees. Revitalised between 1980 and 1981 by the Forest
Service and more recently by the National Trust, the
area is now noted for its Rose Garden whose box-edged
beds contain such varieties as *Rosa* 'White Wing' and
R. 'Mrs Oakley Fisher'. The surrounding bagatelles
support a mixture of climbing roses and clematis with
Dutch lavender below.

The seven-acre Pleasure Grounds to the south of the
house, once known as the American Garden, are
traversed by a network of meandering gravel footpaths
laid down in the 1840s with clumps of shrubs and a
few specimen trees set in a green expanse of mowed
grass. The area is dominated by rhododendrons,
notably cultivars of *R. ponticum* and *R. arboreum* with
some fine specimens of the early hybrid *R.* x *russellia-
num* 'Cornish Red'. A variety of azaleas, viburnums
and dogwoods are dotted around the area in addition
to a range of maples, cherries and medlars. Among the
magnolias is a large *M. virginiana*, while close to the
river at the bottom of the garden are two outstanding
specimens of weeping beech, one of which is now
reaching the end of its life. The variety of plantings on
the stream banks include primula (*P. denticulata*, *P.
pulverulenta* and *P.* 'Rowallane Rose'), large-leaved
hostas, *Dierama pulcherrimum*, rodgersias, and
Curtonus paniculatus which has naturalised itself here.
There are also New Zealand daisies, Solomon's seal,
bergenias, gunnera, peltiphyllums and large astilbes.

The original Florence Court yew, *Taxus baccata*
'Fastigiata', lies about half a mile south east of the
house in the Cottage Wood and is approached by a

path running along the stream from the Pleasure Grounds. Discovered in the 1760s by one of Lord Enniskillen's tenants on the slopes of Cuilcagh Mountain, this tree has an upright rather than spreading habit and can be propagated only from cuttings. As the mother plant of countless millions of Irish yews, no visit to Florence Court could possibly be complete without a pilgrimage to this world-famous tree, even if (in its venerable old age) it has a rather scraggy appearance.

Located 8 miles south west of Enniskillen on the Swanlinbar Road. NGR: H 175343. Park open daily, except 25 December: 10.00 am to one hour before dusk. House open daily, Easter and April to September, except Tuesdays: 1.00 – 6.00 pm. Teas and lunches available (open as Florence Court house). Gift shop. Toilet facilities. Suitable for wheelchairs. Dogs on lead. Admission: £1.00 per car to Forest Park and National Trust garden areas. Entry to the house: adults £2.40; children £1.15. Group rates available upon request. Tel: (036582) 249.

DERREEN

County Kerry

The benign climate of West Cork and Kerry has favoured the development of some outstanding gardens. One of the most verdant of these is the woodland glade garden at Derreen – a subtropical jungle of luxuriant vegetation occupying the whole of a ninety-acre peninsula in a sheltered inlet amidst the splendid setting of the wild and majestic Caha Mountains.

The creation of the garden at Derreen began in 1870 after the fifth Marquis of Landsdowne inherited the house and demesne from his father. Realising the potential of the property with its high rainfall and rare frosts, the young Marquis set about transforming the bare rock and native scrub oak of the peninsula into the garden we see today. For nearly sixty years he devoted himself to the task, spending three months every year at Derreen – excluding the years between 1883 and 1894 when he was Governor General of Canada and Viceroy of India. Because of the excellent growing conditions here, the Marquis had the rare pleasure of witnessing his plantations grow to full maturity.

Derreen is designed around the house – a pleasant, unassuming, mid nineteenth-century building, rebuilt and enlarged in the 1920s after being burnt down in the Civil War. Plush, undulating lawns sweep down from the house to the woodland below. Here, wide grassy vistas give way to a labyrinth of narrow mossy paths which weave their way through groves of bamboo, towering eucalyptus, tree ferns and a wide variety of conifers, some planted as specimens, some in small groups. In their shade dense hedges of gaultheria and pernettya grow so freely they have to be regularly cut back. Kalmia and leptospermum plants thrive here, as do olearias, azaleas, drimys and, above all, the rhododendrons which are found everywhere in profusion – some of enormous size.

Visitors touring the garden begin their journey by passing a huge, dome-shaped rock used in ancient times as a tribal meeting place. The path downslope to the boathouse winds past a variety of myrtaceae including a fine example of *Myrtus luma*, a species from Chile which seeds itself prolifically all over the grounds. This produces white flowers in August as does a sweet-scented pepper bush (*Clethra alnifolia*) growing further down the path. In this area a number of fine rhododendrons from the Himalayas flourish, including a magnificent *R. falconeri* with huge creamy-white bell-shaped flowers and a large *R. sinogrande*, notable for its enormous dark green leaves with their silvery-grey underside.

At the boathouse garden enthusiasts should proceed uphill along the Middle Walk which winds over and around lichen-encrusted rocks and lush vegetation. A short distance to the right, a path leads to Froude's Seat, named after the historian who stayed at Derreen in 1867. Here clumps of *R.* 'Loderi King George' grow – generally considered to be the finest of all the hybrid rhododendrons. Further along the walk are more clusters of fine Himalayan rhododendrons, including *R. niveum*, *R. keysii* and *R. griffithianum*, the latter well known as the parent of innumerable prize-winning hybrids. A handsome *Drimys winteri* also thrives in this area – its fragrant ivory-white flowers filling the air with scent in May.

From the Middle Walk the path north passes an attractive *Thujopsis dolabrata* from Japan with large flattened sprays of silver-backed leaves. Close by an extremely beautiful *Pinus patula* graces the scene, drooping foliage. To the left, the path leads onto the King's Oozy whose twisting course over rocks and down steps brings one to a grove of majestic *Thuja plicata* planted around 1880. Further along this path the visitor will come across the most remarkable feature of the whole garden – a grove of tree ferns from New Zealand, *Dicksonia antarctica*, planted here around 1900. These have become completely naturalised, constantly renewing themselves by self-sown spores (which come up all over the place, particularly in drainage ditches where they grow to enormous sizes). Here, in the shade of jade-stemmed bamboo and a large Tasmanian blue gum, one has the thrilling sensation of walking in a subtropical rain-forest.

Many of the paths in the garden provide marvellous glimpses of the sea and distant mountains, particularly the Broad Walk around the north of the peninsula. On the way back to the house along the Rock Garden Walk visitors will not fail to be impressed with a remarkable specimen of the beautiful Japanese cypress (*Cryptomeria japonica* 'Elegans'). This is one of the largest examples of its kind but thanks to a storm now unhappily lies in a near horizontal position almost blocking the walk. From here the path leads to a grassy glade with a fine Chinese rhododendron, *R. lutescens*, in view of the house. Before departing, a climb up to Knockatee Seat will reward one with a heavenly view.

The garden is presently owned and maintained by the Honourable David Bigham, a decandant of Lord

Landsdowne. It rains often in this lush county, so bring Wellingtons and expect plenty of flies and midges in season.

Located north of Lauragh, 15 miles south west of Kenmare. NGR: V 775585. Open daily, April to October: 11.00 am – 6.00 pm. Parking and picnic area behind the house. Lunches and teas available in tea room. Toilet facilities. Dogs on lead. Admission: adults IR £2.00; children IR £1.00; adult groups of 20+, 10% discount. Tel: (064) 83103. Best season: April to May.

DUNLOE CASTLE GARDENS

County Kerry

The romantic lake and mountain landscape around Killarney has long attracted botanists and plant enthusiasts and the gardens in the grounds of Dunloe Castle Hotel are a particularly rewarding destination. Set in an incomparable location with magnificent panoramic views of the towering MacGillycuddy Reeks, these gardens contain an exceptionally rich variety of trees and shrubs, including many species that are rarely if at all found elsewhere in Ireland.

The basis of the present garden was created between 1922 and 1936 during the ownership of Howard Harrington, an American who was determined to establish an interesting and extensive range of trees and shrubs despite the exposed, elevated position of the site. Creating plenty of windbreaks, he laid down a fine arboretum and utilised the shelter of an old walled garden for a choice collection of plants. His splendid creation was later acquired by Miss Agnes Petitt who lovingly maintained the gardens until her death in 1960. The grounds were subsequently purchased by a German-owned hotel company who decided not only to retain the gardens but to expand them. Accordingly, advice on future planting was sought from the horticulturalists Gerd Krussmann and Roy Lancaster and from Harold Hillier, head of the famous Winchester-based nursery firm. As a result the range of plants at Dunloe has significantly increased over recent decades.

The garden is designed to be approached from the hotel, a large modern complex lying close to the site of Harrington's old house. A straight path leads directly to the Walled Garden, but rather than follow this the serious visitor should venture directly into the arboretum in front of the conference hall. Here some of the most interesting trees and shrubs in the garden are found, including quite a variety of rare maples such as the *Acer laevigatum* with its semi-evergreen leaves and the *A. pectinatum* from the Himalayas, notable for its rich autumn colour. Other curious specimens include the small shrubby hornbeam from Asia, *Carpinus cordata*; a conspicuous white-flowering ash from the Himalayas, *Fraxinus floribunda*; the hybrid hazel *Corylus* x *colournoides*; and a few rare cherry trees from China, including a specimen of *Prunus litigiosa* which the Irish plant hunter Augustine Henry first found at the end of the last century. Another of Henry's introductions, the hornbeam *Carpinus henryana*, can be seen at the other end of the arboretum along with a shagbark hickory notable for its rich yellow autumn leaves and the distinctive but rarely seen conifer from Taiwan, *Calocedrus formosana*.

Before entering the Walled Garden it is worth inspecting the area just behind the shelter where a birch from western China, *Betula albo-sinensis septentrionalis*, proudly displays its shining orange-brown bark with peeling pink and grey blooms. On the other side of the shelter along the path leading into the Walled Garden are a number of camellias, including the tender *C. taliensis*, and the suckering shrub *Clerodendrum bungei* whose rosy-red fragrant flowers send the butterflies into a swoon of ecstasy in late summer.

The Walled Garden is divided into a series of beds and borders containing a fine collection of rhododendrons, magnolias and camellias planted closely beside the fronds of many rare and tender plants. Following the main box-lined path through the garden, the visitor will note a specimen of *Banksia marginata*, an interesting Australian shrub with cone-shaped flower-heads, the Chilean hazel *Gevuina avellana*, a magnificent *Viburnum odoratissimum* from China, and an example of the Californian laurel *Umbellularia californica* whose pungently aromatic leaves, if crushed and inhaled, are liable to produce headaches or faintness. Further along is a good example of the maple *Acer hersii* with its wonderfully marbled bark, while on the opposite side of the path specimens of the New Zealand black pine (*Podocarpus spicatus*) and the South African shrub *Bowkeria gerardiana*, which normally needs to be grown in a conservatory in Ireland, are found.

The north wall of the garden provides a suitable environment for quite a variety of plants: the white-flowering *Eucryphia moorei* from Australia, the magnificent Chilean foliage plant *Lomatia ferruginea*, the remarkable *Camellia granthamiana* from Hong Kong, a species with large parchment-white flowers that is now endangered in the wild. A variety of fine maples also grows here, including a handsome *Acer pentaphyllum* with distinctive fingered leaves and the slow-growing *A. japonicum* 'Aureum' with yellow leaves. In the area to the south a very fine example of the Chinese paperbark maple (*A. griseum*) has been planted; its peeling bark and gorgeous red and scarlet autumnal leaves make this a tree of quite extraordinary beauty.

The path out of the Walled Garden leads to the shell of the old thirteenth-century castle. Close by the visitor will make out a darkly handsome evergreen: the gnarled Killarney strawberry tree (*Arbutus unedo*), native of the woods of Kerry and belonging to the heath family of plants (*Ericaceae*). Its white bell-like flowers and red fruit are produced simultaneously in late autumn. From here the visitor may choose to return to the hotel by a series of paths on the east side of the gardens. In doing so a whole range of shrubs is revealed, including a good example of *Berberis asiatica* from Nepal, the heavily scented *Ozothamnus ledifolius* from Tasmania and the Gippsland waratah (*Telopea oreades*), one of the most exotic and curious of all flowers at Dunloe. An alternative route back from the old castle is to the south west, however, bringing the visitor to Dunloe's greatest treasure: the Chinese pond cypress (*Glyptostrobus lineatus*). This tree has been planted in a sheltered, swampy area of the wood by the river and has grown to a height of nine metres, possibly the largest of its kind in Europe. In theory it should never have survived here but in practice, like so much else at Dunloe, it has successfully defied the gods.

Located 5 miles west of Killarney and 1 mile south of Beauford. NGR: V 808901. Open daily: May to October. Groups and tours by appointment. Catalogue available in hotel for IR £1.00. Toilet facilities. Suitable for wheelchairs. Dogs on lead. Admission: free. Tel: (064) 31900/44111.

TULLY JAPANESE GARDENS

County Kildare

Normally gardens consult the genius of place in their design but at Tully the local countryside is excluded and the visitor enters an environment that exudes the mystical and botanical world of distant Japan. One of the most successful gardens of its kind, Tully is a product of the Edwardian vogue for Japanese garden-making which developed as part of a movement away from the English garden and in response to a rage for autumn colour and a ready availability of a wide variety of maples.

The gardens were devised and subsequently presented to the nation by Colonel Hall-Walker, later Lord Wavertree, a wealthy businessman, orientalist and successful albeit capricious horse-breeder who had established a stud at Tully. He imported a shipload of plants, bonsai, stone ornaments and even a geisha house from Japan and employed a Japanese landscape designer, Tassa Eida, who travelled to Ireland with his wife and two sons and lived at Kildare from 1906 to 1910, to supervise the work of forty Irish gardeners.

The constituent elements of a Japanese garden are characteristically used in a symbolic composition to express an idea. At Tully the designer has made the path through the garden symbolical of the vicissitudes of man's life from the cradle to the grave.

The journey starts at the Gate of Oblivion where the soul strives to inhabit a body. Birth is symbolised by a rock cave, followed by a path through a dark tunnel signifying the ignorance and incomprehension of the infant. The growing child may ascend the Hill of Learning, after which he will follow a winding stream where a three-way parting of roads offers a choice between a straight path, indicating bachelorhood, a path lined with cherry trees, indicating a life of self-indulgence, or a middle path leading to the Island of Joy and Wonder with marriage as its reward. The steep Hill of Ambition is climbed and eventually, after a number of blind paths, both married partners enter the Garden of Peace and Contentment with its level lawn, shady trees and wide, slow-moving stream. The Gateway of Eternity brings the pilgrimage to a close.

The gardens are now in the possession of the Irish National Stud and are maintained in an impeccable condition.

Located 1 mile east of Kildare and 25 miles south west of Dublin in Tully. NGR: N 735109. Open daily, June, July and August: 11.00 am – 6.00 pm. Easter to October (omitting above 3 months): Saturdays, 10.00 am – 6.00 pm; Sundays, 2.00 – 6.00 pm. Refreshments available. Gift shop. Plants for sale. Toilet facilities. Admission to gardens, Irish National Stud and Horse Museum: adults IR £4.00; senior citizens and students IR £3.00; children under 12 IR £2.00. Tel: (045) 21617.

EMO COURT

County Leix

Some gardens deserve to be better known and those at Emo Court are a prime example. Covering fifty-five acres, they include spreading lawns, marvellous statuary, leafy shrubs, a wealth of fine trees, a lake and a series of attractive walks, each with a different theme to explore. The focus of the gardens is a monumental neo-classical country house by the celebrated Irish architect James Gandon, built in 1790 for John Dawson, the first Earl of Portarlington. Emo was sold in 1930 to the Jesuits who used it as a noviciate and later in 1969 to the present owner, Mr C. D. Cholmeley-Harrison, who has not only carried out a remarkable restoration of the house but has restored the gardens admirably, planting a considerable number of new trees and shrubs.

The garden is divided into two main parts: the Clucker and the much larger Grapery. The Clucker, an area of light woodland, lies behind the yard and is seen first by visitors. It contains some of the garden's finest trees, including large examples of *Cedrus deodara*, *Pinus radiata* and *Picea smithiana*. Beneath the tree canopy there is a wide selection of azaleas and rhododendrons as well as a variety of other shrubs such as potentilla, some in strip beds alongside the paths. The area looks at its best in spring but there are plenty of lithe maples to give colour in autumn.

Avenues of dignified Florence Court yews planted in Victorian times criss-cross broad stretches of lawn around the house. The great formal parterres have long since gone but some fine statues remain, including four depicting the seasons. Beyond statues of Persephone and Flora, a path brings the visitor down to the lake passing through a large collection of camellias on the way. The late eighteenth-century lake, some twenty acres in extent, has been invaded with weeds in recent years but its perimeter is attractively planted with trees and shrubs which look particularly lovely in autumn when *Parrotia persica*, among other plants, display their amber and scarlet glow.

A collection of maples provides more glorious autumn colour along the route to the Grapery – a large and exceptionally beautiful arboretum. Crossed by a series of walks with such evocative names as the Everglade, the Apiary Walk and the Via Davidia, this great expanse is dotted with a large collection of specimen trees through which a vista runs aligned upon the distant mansion. Avenues of very old lime and beech closer to the house are residual elements of an early eighteenth-century formal layout that was associated with Dawson's Court – the house which pre-dated the present Emo Court. An impressive folly on a distant hill in the park, now hidden by trees, also belongs to this early period in the demesne's history.

The front of Emo Court is not seen by visitors to the gardens. Aligned upon this façade is a mile-long avenue of Wellingtonias (*Sequoiadendron giganteum*), all planted in the mid 1850s and undoubtedly the finest of their kind to be found anywhere in the British Isles. When Edward VII came here in the early part of this century, the entire length of this avenue was lined with a jubilee carpet!

Located 6 miles south of Portlaoise. NGR: N 539066. Open daily: 10.30 am – 5.30 pm. House open 15 March – 18 October, Mondays only: 2.00 – 6.00 pm. Tea, scones and cake available in the old pump house. Toilet facilities. Suitable for wheelchairs. No dogs. Admission: adults IR £2.00; senior citizens, students and children IR £1.00. Admission to house: IR £2.50. Combined ticket to house and gardens: IR £3.50. Tel: (0502) 26110.

HEYWOOD

County Leix

In 1906 the famous English architect and garden designer Sir Edward Lutyens (1869–1944) was commissioned by Colonel Hutcheson Poë to design a garden for his grand Georgian house at Heywood, where decades previously the Empress Elizabeth of Austria had been entertained. Work began in 1909 and continued until late 1912, while a planting scheme was prepared for the borders in 1910 by Gertrude Jekyll. Heywood was sold to the Salesian Fathers in 1941 who established their Missionary College here, but in 1950 the house was accidentally burned down and subsequently demolished. The garden remained, its structure gradually decaying until 1985 when a restoration programme was undertaken on its walls and ornaments. A plan to restore the planting in Jekyll's style (her original plans were lost) was prepared by Graham Stuart Thomas – this has been partly implemented with voluntary help and will now be continued by the Office of Public Works who has recently taken over the care of the gardens along with the demesne's eighteenth-century lakes and woodland.

The garden is reached at the end of a long avenue that winds through an elegant landscape park laid out during the 1770s in the romantic-poetic tradition. Passing a Gothic folly made from stonework stolen from a local friary, the visitor arrives at the site of the old house – sadly now a car park set in front of an unappealing modern building. The garden lies just below the south side of the car park and is composed of three separate elements linked by a terrace that once fronted the house.

Visitors enter the garden through a series of small compartments or 'garden rooms' planted with herbaceous plants and delimited by clipped yew hedges. From here a curving staircase leads down into a large elliptical garden where three terraced borders drop to a central oval pond encircling a large stone fountain. At the east end stands a pavilion with a steep pantile roof, while at the opposite end an elegant gateway leads into an alley of pleached limes. Beyond this lies a large flat terrace with a lawn and borders that were once overlooked by the house windows. At the far end of this lawn a flight of steps arrives at a pergola terrace, whose oak beams are supported by Ionic columns taken from one of the eighteenth-century follies in the park. The pergola was once wreathed with wisteria and

Water lily in Italian garden, Heywood

roses, while narrow flower beds between the columns contained fuchsias and hydrangeas. Now only cascades of *Clematis tangutica* grow here, but the views of the park and its lake below are quite lovely and a fitting climax to this splendid garden.

Located 3 miles from Abbeyleix, just outside Ballinakill. NGR: S 472817. Open daily, May to August: 11.00 am – 6.00 pm or by appointment. Partly suitable for wheelchairs. Dogs on lead. Admission: adults IR £2.00; students and children IR £1.00. Tel: (0502) 33334.

THE GUY WILSON
DAFFODIL GARDEN

County L'Derry

Although the genus *Narcissus* is not native to Ireland, few countries can lay greater claim to this most heavenly of spring flowers – the daffodil. From the period when hybridisation first began over a century ago, Irish breeders have led the world in the number and quality of cultivars raised. As a tribute to these hybridists, a daffodil collection has been established in the grounds of the University of Ulster at Coleraine where the products of their efforts are preserved for future breeders and enthusiasts. The garden is dedicated to the memory of Guy L. Wilson of Broughshane, (1885–1962) one of the country's leading hybridists and the man who did most to develop daffodil breeding in Ireland over the past fifty years.

The collection occupies the site of an old quarry on the south side of the campus at Fortview, close to the Portstewart Road. The setting is attractive with its south-facing lawns, informal paths, irregular-shaped island beds of shrubs interplanted with daffodils, and a large drift providing a magnificent splash of colour in the centre of the layout. The first planting of bulbs took place in 1971 and amounted to 165 cultivars, embedded in clumps of twenty or more. In 1974 the garden was opened to the public and in the years following the collection was expanded enormously under the guidance of Dr David Willis, then the University grounds superintendent. Donations of bulbs from as far afield as New Zealand, Holland, the US as well as Britain have enlarged the collection to its present number of around 1,500 old and modern cultivars.

A major proportion of the cultivars in the collection are the creation of Irish breeders, notably J. Lionel Richardson, W. J. Dunlop and Tom Bloomer. The Guy Wilson cultivars are principally represented by white daffodils with which he achieved his greatest fame and success. Wilson's name is especially associated with white trumpet daffodils, and visitors to the garden can seek out such early award-winning jewels as 'White Dame', 'Driven Snow' and 'Everest' and his later triumphs: 'Kanchenjunga', 'Cantatrice', 'Empress of Ireland' and 'Rasheen'. He also achieved fame for his large-cupped whites, notably 'Slemish' and 'Ava', once described as one of the most perfect flowers in cultivation, while the small-cupped 'Chinese White' is perhaps one of the most successful daffodils ever produced. Wilson was interested in reverse bicolours and played a major role in developing the revolutionary 'Spellbinder' cultivar with its unusual colour combinations of yellow perianth and white trumpet. He also tried to develop pink varieties, but it was his great contemporary Lionel Richardson of Waterford who had the most success with pinks, producing such world beaters as 'Rose Caprice', 'Infatuation', 'Salome' and 'Romance'. Richardson experimented with double-flowered daffodils and in later years produced many commendable yellow trumpet varieties, including 'Kingscourt' and 'King's Ransom'. Contemporary Irish daffodil breeders are represented in the collection as well; here we are offered glimpses of Kate Reade's pink 'Foundling' and Brian Duncan's superb double 'Pink Pagent'.

Visitors should note that there are many other daffodils on display around the campus, flowering in drifts on lawns and in the New Garden close to the main roundabout. In recent years a combination of university cut-backs and vandalism has put this collection in serious jeopardy, but the future now seems more secure under the present management though a great deal more public support is needed to upgrade this sublime collection.

Located 1 mile north of Coleraine on the Portstewart Road (A2) at the University of Ulster, Coleraine. NGR: C 847339. Open from dawn to dusk, all year. Parking at the Marina. Dogs on lead. Admission: free. Tel: (0265) 44141. Best season: April.

BUTTERSTREAM

County Meath

Some gardens offer an exciting journey of discovery, slowly unfurling their secrets and charms to the visitor. Butterstream does not at first give the impression of being a sizable garden, but gradually reveals itself through a series of interlinking compartments, each devoted to different arrangements of plants. There is a rose garden, a white garden, a wild garden, an herbaceous garden, a pool garden and many others, all containing wonderfully controlled masses of flower and leaf forms hidden away by neatly clipped hedges and leafy screens.

Although the garden has a venerable appearance, Butterstream only began life during the 1970s when Jim Reynolds started to transform the farmland between his family home and the adjacent stream. As an archaeologist based in Mullingar, Reynolds could devote only evenings and weekends to the task but still managed by his own efforts to reclaim two and a half acres of heavy limestone clay in this dank part of Ireland into a remarkable garden in the tradition of Hidcote and Sissinghurst – fulfilling Vita Sackville-West's ideal of 'the strictest formality of design, with the maximum informality in planting'.

The first area to be created was the Rose Garden – a long rectangular compartment with beech surround and box-hedging flanking beds each side of a central path. The box-hedges are clipped higher than one might normally expect as the roses are old-fashioned varieties whose lanky legs need to be hidden. This large collection includes many varieties of Gallica, Damask, Bourbon, Alba and moss roses that Jim Reynolds has collected over the years from garden centres, old gardens and even roadside verges. Among these is the vigorous moss rose 'Gloire des Mousseux' and the late nineteenth-century hybrid perpetual 'Souvenir du Dr Jamain', discovered by Vita Sackville-West in an abandoned corner of a nursery in the south of England and later brought into cultivation. Beneath the roses, lilies, crinum, nerine and clematis have been planted to extend the season of the garden.

From here a path leads into a smaller adjacent compartment – the White Garden – another early feature of the layout. It too has paths bordered by neatly clipped boxwood hedges and these contain white forms of agapanthus, delphiniums, astrantias and campanulas, as well as green-and-white striped reed Canary grass, white *Clematis recta* and a tall but elegant meadow rue (*Thalictrum delavayi*). In the corner an attractive round tower with sprocketed roof, resembling for all the world an ancient dove-cote, has recently been built as a look-out over the garden. Close by the path has been lined with white petunias, many trailing freely out of large clay pots and making a glorious impact in late summer.

On the opposite side of the Rose Garden lies another even smaller compartment, the Red and Yellow Garden, also delimited by tall clipped beech hedges. This little area has been reserved for all the vibrant colours – the reds, scarlets, yellows and strident oranges that are rather difficult to mix in borders to good effect. Some of the most startling come from the day lilies – the golden-yellows of *Hemerocallis* 'Golden Chimes' and the brilliant reds of *H.* 'Stafford'. Here the tiny vermillion flowers of the Maltese cross (*Lychnis chalcedonica*), the large daisy-like bright orange heads of *Ligularia dentata* 'Desdemona', and masses of heleniums all provide vivid colour from midsummer to autumn, while the sword-shaped erect leaves of a variety of crocosmia instil an exotic touch. The tropical feeling is increased by bronze-leaved phormiums and yellow grasses. Towering above is a lovely *Robinia* 'Frisia' whose leaves catch the light spectacularly even on a dull day.

Herbaceous borders at Butterstream

The Woodland Garden occupies a sizable area beyond the Red and Yellow compartment. The emphasis here is on foliage variations and hostas predominate with no less than sixty-five varieties represented. They are grown in great masses and give a wave-like effect beneath the trees. An exotic wooden structure surmounted by a pineapple has been built at one end of this garden, while a handsome Gothick bridge bends across the adjacent stream, its banks planted with drifts of primulas.

The centre-piece of Butterstream is the large Herbaceous Garden. This has an oval island bed with a surrounding grass path and is planted magnificently – a rare sight in Ireland these days. The large beds, thirty-feet wide and one hundred-feet long, contain a wide choice of herbaceous perennials such as lobelia, macleaya, kniphofia, allium and phlox, all yielding a good succession of colour from late June to late October. They are planted in bold clumps and arranged in marvellous colour schemes that range from yellows to blues to mauves, pinks and plenty of whites, with the severer colours left out. Some plants to note are the thistle-like *Eryngium* x *zabelii* 'Slieve Donard', the violet blue-flowering *Salvia nemorosa* 'East Friesland', the lovely pink-flowering *Potentilla nepalensis* 'Miss Willmott', and the tall branching spikes and pink-buff flowers of the coral plume, *Macleaya microcarpa*, at the back of the borders.

A large rectangular lawn extends beyond the herbaceous borders with flanking shrubs, tall trees, deep purple hedges and a rustic bower, providing a contrast to the strong colours and confined spaces of other parts of the garden. Close by a laburnum-clad pergola leads into the cool atmosphere of an Italian garden, reflected in a rectangular pool replete with water lilies and carp. Here in the little classical pavilion visitors can relax and – in late summer – watch the white flowers of *Epilobium angustifolium album* dance beneath this sylvan scene.

Located just outside Trim on the Kildalkey Road. NGR: N 797572. Open daily, May to September, except Mondays: 2.00 – 6.00 pm. Plants for sale. Suitable for wheelchairs. Admission: adults IR £3.00; children IR £1.00. Tel: (046) 36017.

BIRR CASTLE GARDENS

County Offaly

Hornbeam allées in the formal gardens at Birr

The gardens at Birr Castle, though large by any standards, exude an atmosphere of intimacy as well as grandeur. They extend across 150 acres of an eighteenth-century 'Brownian' demesne park whose lake, rivers, woodlands and sweeping open spaces are adorned by an outstanding collection of nearly 2,000 species of rare trees and shrubs, many grown from seed collected in the wild. Some of Birr's varied delights include the Walled Garden with its impressive formal layout, the Victorian Fernery, the Lagoon Garden, an arboretum, the High Walk and the River Walk, while the focus of the whole layout is the splendid Gothicised castle which stands with its back to the town gazing out over the parkland above Vaubanesque fortifications and terraces. Birr's best-known feature is undoubtedly the great Gothic frame of the 'Leviathan', the world's largest nineteenth-century telescope – one of the many achievements of a remarkable family whose varied tastes over fourteen successive generations are reflected in the development of this magnificent parkland garden.

During medieval times the castle and demesne of Birr belonged to the O'Carroll's, rulers of Ely O'Carroll, a territory covering about 160 square miles. In 1620 it was granted to Sir Laurence Parsons, an English adventurer who had made good in Ireland. Parsons laid the foundations of the town and built the core of the present castle which was later reconstructed and enlarged after suffering damage during the wars of the seventeenth century.

The park began to assume its present appearance in 1778 when Sir William Parsons began digging the lake and planting beech trees in the prevailing landscape style of the time. This work was continued by his son Sir Lawrence Parsons (1758–1841), an enlightened and liberal-minded patriot who became the second Earl of Rosse upon the death of an uncle in 1807. Much of his energy was devoted to improving Birr after he retired from politics in 1800, disheartened with the Act of Union. He turned the old house back to front so it faced the park, heightened and crenellated it in the Gothick style, laid out a new avenue, built the suspension bridge over the River Camcor, created the Walled Garden as it exists today, and planted a great many trees. If lack of money ever limited the demesne's development, it certainly ceased to be a factor after 1836 when the property was inherited by his son William, the third Earl of Rosse (1800–1867). William's wife Mary was heiress of the Fields of Heaton outside Bradford and it was with her enormous fortune that the third Earl was able to build his famous telescope between 1841 and 1844. During the Potato Famine the Countess financed the employment of over 500 men in the demesne – enlarging the lake, constructing the stable block and the keep gate, and digging the massive mock military-style 'star fort' in front of the castle, designed by her uncle Colonel Myddleton, a veteran of the Peninsula War campaign. An impressive fernery was built in the 1850s but after this no new additions were added to the demesne for over half a century.

While the third and fourth earls of Rosse were principally interested in astronomy and engineering, the fifth and sixth earls were devoted to developing the gardens at Birr. After he inherited in 1908, the fifth Earl flattened the moat between the castle and the river to make garden terraces and planted fine trees and shrubs along the banks of the Camcor, including a collection he had purchased at the sale of Sir Harry Veitch's famous London nursery in 1914. Included within this collection were a number of Wilson introductions from China; an exceptionally rare *Carrierea calycina*, specimens of *Rhododendron yunnanense* and a very fine *Magnolia delavayi* still survive today.

No doubt it was the presence of such plants at Birr that inspired the young sixth Earl of Rosse, who succeeded his father in 1918, to develop an interest in botany and to become a renowned horticulturalist and plantsman. His outstanding achievements in not only enriching the park with many rare trees and shrubs but also in furthering the aims of conservation in both Ireland and Great Britain are commemorated in a small tree from North Korea (*Euodia daniellii*) lying close to the garden entrance. The Himalayas and the Far East were, in fact, his principal areas of interest and in his pursuit of new material he insisted on obtaining plants of known wild origin or cultivars of the very highest quality. Accordingly he sponsored and subscribed to plant collecting expeditions and visited China together with his wife in 1935. When he died in 1979 at the age of seventy-two, he left behind one of Ireland's greatest gardens brimming with Wilson, Forrest, Kingdon-Ward, Henry, Rock and Yü Tse-Tsun introductions. The garden is now being maintained and enlarged by his son and successor, the seventh Earl of Rosse, who has continued to associate Birr with plant collecting expeditions, notably those of Lancaster and Rushforth, and has himself participated in an expedition to Nepal.

In order to get a feel for the geography and planting of Birr, visitors should head straight for the River Garden, passing the massive ramparts below the castle. Here in the garden's heartland along the banks of the River Camcor some of Birr's most prized plants can be found, perhaps none more beautiful than a tender collection of magnolias cushioned by a blue carpet of *Omphalodes cappadocica* in spring. Varieties of magnolia include the pink-flowering *M. dawsoniana*, the fragrant white-flowering *M. officinalis* and the spectacular varieties of *M. veitchii*, *M. heptapeta* and *M. sprengeri*. Equally striking is the large specimen of *M.*

delavayi growing against the terrace walls which was supplied by Veitch just before the outbreak of the Great War. Quite a number of the magnolias here were raised from seeds collected at Nymans, one of England's greatest gardens and home of Anne, Countess of Rosse, wife of the sixth Earl. Here also is the magnificent white-flowering *Eucryphia* x *nymansensis* 'Nymansay', while other gems along the river bank include the rare *Carrierea calycina* from western China, a Cork oak (*Quercus suber*) and the largest known example of a

Peony 'Anne Rosse' in the walled garden at Birr

grey poplar (*Populus canescens*). The suspension bridge over the river, built in 1810, is the earliest of its kind known in Ireland.

On the High Walk above the River Garden visitors will come across a large specimen of the rare Chinese tree *Ehretia dicksonii*, characterised by its broad corymbs of small fragrant white flowers in June. Here in this thicket a large London plane also thrives, and beyond lies a Morinda spruce flanking the Lilac Walk. The northerly path alongside the lake passes a weeping beech, a large Pacific dogwood (*Cornus nuttallii*) and a dawn redwood (*Metasequoia glyptostroboides*) – a remarkable deciduous conifer discovered in 1941 and known previously only from fossils millions of years old. This specimen, one of two plants received from Kew, is among the earliest in cultivation.

The arboretum on the Tipperary side of the river is divided by an avenue of recently planted *Prunus* 'Accolade', noted for their pendulous clusters of semi double-pink flowers. Within the arboretum are many trees of distinction, including an excellent oriental beech (*Fagus orientalis*), young examples of the limes *Tilia henryana* and *T. chingiana* and many fine conifers: a *Larix laricina* and *Thuja plicata*. Crossing back over the bridge into the Offaly part of the demesne, visitors have the option of walking straight on towards the Walled Garden or taking a detour to visit the Fernery. The latter option is recommended, for this restored Victorian fernery with its little bridges, jets of water and moss-covered rocks is one of the finest examples of its kind to survive in the British Isles. North of the Fernery is a recently built well, lavishly decorated with sea shells.

The Walled Garden is divided into a kitchen garden to the north and an ornamental area to the south. On the main north-south axis of the garden an impressive pair of thirty-foot-high box hedges – planted over 200 years ago and claimed in the *Guinness Book of Records* to be the tallest in the world – looms upwards. The south-east quarter of the garden contains a suite of formal gardens laid out by Anne, Countess of Rosse, to mark her marriage in 1935. Central to this layout is a boxwood parterre centered around a pair of baroque urns and based on a Bavarian seventeenth-century garden design. This is enclosed by cloisters of pleached hornbeam allées with ceilings of curving baroque forms aligned upon statues of the Graces and bordered with winter-flowering snowdrops. Flanking the old greenhouse to one side is the wisteria garden which, in addition to the venerable wisteria *W. floribunda* 'Macrobotrys', contains the oldest and one of the finest magnolias at Birr: *M. stellata* from Japan, planted around 1910 and now over twenty feet in diameter. A few yards away lies an exceptionally fine specimen of the Japanese bitter orange tree (*Poncirus trifoliata*) whose scented white flowers bloom endlessly in May.

Before leaving the Walled Garden, visitors should seek out Birr's most famous plant: *Paeonia* 'Anne Rosse' – a tree peony with large ruffled yellow flowers, streaked with red. It is named after Anne, the late Dowager Countess of Rosse, and was a hybrid (created by her husband) between a yellow tree peony discovered in south-eastern Tibet (*P. lutea ludlowii*) and a Chinese Yü introduction (*P. delavayi*) which has small flowers of dark red. It won an award of merit and the Cory Cup and, perhaps more than any other plant, symbolises the profound contribution that Birr and the sixth Earl of Rosse have made to Irish horticulture.

Magnolia *'Michael Rosse', Birr*

Located in the town of Birr. NGR: N 056047. Open daily, January to March and November to December: 9.00 am – 1.00 pm and 2.00 – 5.00 pm. April to October: 9.00 am – 6.00 pm (or dusk when earlier). Parking in street outside gates. Refreshments and teas outside castle gates. Gift shop. Plants for sale. Toilet facilities. Suitable for wheelchairs. Dogs on lead. Exhibition from 1 May to 2 October featuring the making of the gardens. Castle not open. Admission: January to March and November to December: adults IR £2.60; children IR £1.30. April to October: adults IR £3.20; children IR £1.60; adults in groups of 20+ IR £2.60; children in groups of 20+ IR £1.30. Admission free for children under 5 and for fourth and subsequent children of families with more than three children. Annual subscriptions: families IR £30.00; individuals IR £15.00. Tel: (0509) 20056. Property of the year, 1993.

LISMORE CASTLE GARDENS

County Waterford

In the turbulent centuries preceding the reign of Charles II most substantial Irish gardens were protected behind walled or embanked enclosures adjacent to a house or castle. The Upper Garden at Lismore is a splendid surviving example of such an early garden – notable not only for its impressive walls, turrets and terracing but also because it has remained in continuous use for over three-and-a-half centuries. Its appeal is perhaps increased by the tradition that Spencer wrote part of his *Faerie Queen* here.

The gardens are entered through an outer gatehouse known as the Riding House, built in 1631 to provide accommodation for mounted horsemen. The old Upper Garden lies to the left of the avenue and occupies a large rectangular area on two terraces. Its surrounding walls were built in 1626 by Richard Boyle, the Great Earl of Cork, a remarkable Elizabethan adventurer who had acquired the castle from Sir Walter Raleigh in 1602. In his diary he records payments by his mother 'for compassing my orchard and garden at Lismore

Main path through upper garden, Lismore

with a wall of two and half feet thick and fourteen feet high of lyme and stone and two turrets at each corner' and later recorded paying for 'digging, mowing and laying my terrace with paved, hewn stones in all over one hundred and six feet'.

Visitors are greeted in the garden by newly planted fruit trees covering part of the area once occupied by the Great Earl's orchard. A central walk between herbaceous borders backed by clipped yew hedges passes through the lower terrace in dramatic alignment with the cathedral spire. This leads to the upper terrace where there are large areas of vegetables. At the north-west end lies a ridge-furrow greenhouse designed by Sir Joseph Paxton in 1858, while in the south-west corner, providing excellent views of the surrounding landscape, a tower looms.

The staircase to the Riding House links the Upper Garden at Lismore with the Victorian pleasure grounds known as the Lower Garden. This area was created around 1850 by the sixth Duke of Devonshire (1770–1858), known as the Bachelor Duke, whose family had inherited Lismore in 1748 when the fourth Duke married Lady Charlotte Boyle, the only daughter and heiress of the fourth Earl of Cork. The principal feature of this garden is an ancient yew walk said to have been planted in 1707 perhaps as an avenue to one of the town houses which formerly occupied the area. The surrounding lawns contain an interesting collection of spring-flowering shrubs, notably camellias, magnolias and rhododendrons including some extremely old specimens of *R. barbatum*, *R. campanulatum*, *R. thomsonii* and *R. falconeri* – possibly planted during the time of the Bachelor Duke. Many improvements have been made to Lismore in recent decades by the present owner, Andrew Cavendish, the eleventh Duke of Devonshire, and visitors will not be disappointed.

Located in the town of Lismore. NGR: X 043987. Open daily, 10 May to 10 September, except Saturdays: 1.45 – 4.45 pm. Admission: adults IR £2.00; children under 16 IR £1.00. For groups of 20+, admission: adults IR £1.70; children IR £0.80. Tel: (058) 54424.

BELVEDERE

County Westmeath

Among the surviving parks that still border the banks of Lough Ennel is Belvedere – perhaps the finest small-scale landscape park in Ireland. Created as the setting for an exquisite villa, it featured a house that was built in 1740 for Robert Rochfort, first Earl of Belvedere, to a design by the celebrated architect Richard Castle. The park is best known for its follies but it also shelters an attractive walled garden and some fine trees.

Belvedere House stands on a knoll facing south west with three formal mid nineteenth-century terraces complete with urns and yews dropping to the waters of the lake and giving panoramic views of Lough Ennel, its woods and islands. Within the rolling parkland, dotted with clumps of trees and distant wooded belts, stand some fine mature trees, notably at the south end below the house where there is a magnificent group of weeping beech, redwood, thuja cedar, sweet chestnut and Douglas fir.

The view south is blocked by the remarkable Jealous Wall, the largest Gothick folly in Ireland. Comprising an enormous sham ruin with pointed windows, it was built to blot out all sight of the neighbouring house, then occupied by the Earl of Belvedere's brother with whom he had violently quarrelled. The folly may be the work of Thomas Wright of Durham (1711–86), the English astronomer and adviser on many gardens who was working in Ireland during the 1740s. Another folly at the northern end of the park, the Gothick Arch, is certainly based on one of Wright's published drawings. An octagonal gazebo built on a fortified terrace of brick and stone is a later construction.

The fine rectangular seven-acre Walled Garden to the east of the house was built by Lieutenant Colonel Charles Howard-Bury who inherited the demesne in 1912. Howard-Bury was a noted traveller and amateur plant collector whose name is commemorated in the white primula *P. buryana* which he brought back to Kew from the Himalayas. Prior to his death in the 1960s the Walled Garden featured impressive herbaceous borders and greenhouses. Many of his plants still grow here – for example, a blue thistle-like echinops, a thirty-three-foot high trachycarpus, shrubs of *Decaisnea fargesii*, clumps of bamboo, and a water-lily pool surrounded by bergenias. Today the garden also grows old roses, hydrangeas and beds containing a range of herbaceous material, all maintained by Westmeath County Council who own the property. It is to be hoped that plans by the council to convert this beautiful demesne into a Disney-style fun park are not realised.

Located 4 miles from Mullingar on the Tullamore Road. NGR: N 420477. Open May to September: 12.00 – 6.00 pm. Refreshments available on Sundays. Toilet facilities. Mostly suitable for wheelchairs. Dogs on lead. Admission: adults IR £1.00; children IR £0.50. Tel: (044) 40861/ 42820.

Rhododendrons in full bloom

JOHN F. KENNEDY
ARBORETUM

County Wexford

A good tree collection is always instructive for the gardener but the J. F. Kennedy Arboretum is particularly enlightening – a marvellous place to learn about and admire the diversity of trees throughout the year. The scale of planting here is on a vast scale, covering 623 acres on the southern slopes of Slieve Coillte, a prominent hill overlooking the Kennedy ancestral home at Dunganstown. Although a very modern venture, for planting began here only in 1964, its ever increasing collection of over 4,500 species of trees and shrubs from the temperate regions, ranging from conifers to flowering shrubs, is now becoming one of the most comprehensive of its kind in the world.

First-time visitors to the arboretum are best to begin at the reception centre, a rather inapposite municipal building lying close to the main car park. Here maps showing the location of different species in the collection can be inspected and a route planned. The layout reflects the underlying function of the arboretum as a research institution. Around 150 acres are divided into 250 forest plots, each devoted to a particular tree species and grouped together geographically. The remaining area of 310 acres is occupied by the plant collection which is laid out in botanical sequence with three examples of every species represented. Each plant is recorded on a grid system, has its own record card and is well labelled. There are two botanical circuits, one of *Gymnospermae* (conifers), the other of *Angiospermae* (broadleaves); the groups have been cleverly interwoven to improve the appearance of the collection by providing colour throughout the year.

Visitors should anticipate a walk of at least two miles around the main circular route, while demon dendrologists may find themselves trekking ten miles or more. Taking the principal arboretum road eastwards from the visitor centre, enthusiasts should inspect the Phenological Garden on the left where the relationship between climate and biological phenomena, such as plant flowering, is researched. Further along, the eucalyptus collection on the other side of the walk has yet to be completed; it includes some fine varieties: *E. cordata* with its smooth white bark and *E. nirens*, the silver-top gum.

Passing through groves of silver fir, the visitor

arrives next at the Ericaceous Garden which occupies much of the eastern part of the arboretum. In addition to a wide variety of heathers, pieris and other peat-loving plants, there are more than 500 rhododendron species and hybrids in this area. These constitute a splendid collection, all presented in an inventive way with something for all seasons.

In the southern sector of the arboretum the walk curves around a small lake; here a lush display of waterside plants and an island of gunnera greet the eye. On the east side of the lake above the main path are many fine magnolias, while on the opposite side lies an extensive collection of cherries providing a glorious mass of colour in early spring. A pleasant walk can be made through the cherries, beyond which is an impressive vista up to the reception centre. The main route, however, goes further south, passing an array of cotoneasters as well as many crataegus and sorbus varieties.

The rocky Alpine Garden, covering about one acre, is the main feature in the western sector of the arboretum. This bed contains a colourful planting of over 320 varieties of dwarf and slow-growing conifers which should not be missed. Further north an extensive area of maple cultivars and a good poplar collection have been laid out. Here in the North-East American plots, the Eastern American plots and the South American and Australian plots conifers and other species of trees enjoy the high sun-duration of this part of Ireland. A drive to the summit of Slieve Coillte to a viewing station at 630 feet will give a magnificent panorama of the whole arboretum and the countryside beyond – a fitting end to a rewarding expedition.

The arboretum was originally established by the State Forestry Division in liaison with the National Botanic Gardens. It is presently administered by Coillte Teoranta – the Irish Forestry Board.

Located 7 miles south of New Ross. NGR: S 729193. Open all year, except 25 December and Good Friday. May to August: 10.00 am – 8.00 pm. April and September: 10.00 am – 6.30 pm. October to March: 10.00 am – 5.00 pm. Café and gift shop open May to September (Sundays only in March – October). Guided tours on weekdays by arrangement. Pony and trap transport and miniature railway open during summer season. Visitor centre with audio-visual presentation. Toilet facilities. Suitable for wheelchairs. Dogs on lead. Admission: adults IR £1.00; family IR £3.00; car season ticket IR £15.00; coach IR £12.00; minibus IR £6.00. Tel: (051) 88171. Best season: April to July.

JOHNSTOWN CASTLE

County Wexford

The harmony between great Victorian revival castles and their surrounding ornamental grounds is rarely seen to such perfection as at Johnstown. The mature woodlands and lakes of this demesne provide the perfect setting for this turreted, battlemented and machicolated castle of gleaming silver-grey ashlar, built for the Grogan-Morgan family between 1810 and 1855 and incorporating part of a more ancient castle. The property was presented as a gift to the Nation in 1945 and was later occupied by the Department of Agriculture who established an agricultural institute here and undertook to maintain but not to alter the ornamental grounds.

The Kilkenny architect Daniel Robertson, who was responsible for some of the building work on the castle, is generally believed to have laid out and planted much of the grounds in the 1830s. This would have included the digging of the five-acre lake opposite the castle with Gothic towers rising from its waters and a terrace lined with statues on the opposite bank. Many fine trees and shrubs grow in the vicinity of the castle, including two lovely examples of *Cryptomeria japonica* 'Elegans', several very fine redwoods (*Sequoia sempervirens*), a huge *Rhododendron arboreum* and some of the oldest and largest specimens of Monterey cypress (*Cupressus macrocarpa*) in Ireland. The variety of mixed planting around the lake, which includes noble firs, Japanese cedars, Atlantic blue cedars, copper beeches, golden Lawson cypresses and holm oaks, provides a very satisfying range of colour through much of the year.

In the area to the west of the castle lake, visitors will pass through a woodland garden created around the ruined medieval castle of Rathlannon. Here the exotic foliage of a *Magnolia wilsonii* from China borders a large, elegant dogwood (*Cornus kousa*) from Japan and a Japanese snowball (*Viburnum plicatum*) with tiered spreading branches. Nearby lies a two-acre lake dug in the 1860s, while in the area to the north is a four-acre walled garden built between 1844 and 1851 and rehabilitated by the Department of Agriculture. This is entered through the Devil's Gate, an arched gateway with gargoyles that leads onto a very long gravel path lined with flower borders and backed by clipped hedges. To the right across mowed lawns a long hothouse shelters a colourful display of plants throughout the year. Steps lead to the Upper Garden, now largely devoted to shrub propagation, and the old melon yard. Here no one will fail to admire a tender dwarf Japanese maple planted in the 1880s and a range of azaleas, magnolias and hibiscus.

Other attractions at Johnstown include a cemetery with very fine wrought-iron gates made in Italy, the site of the sunken Italian Garden close to the car park, and the lower lake, dug in the 1850s and covering some fourteen acres. All three lakes in the demesne provide a home for a wide range of waterfowl – mute swans, moorhens, coots, little grebes, herons and a recently introduced flock of mallards – all of which help to control the waterweeds. The attractive early nineteenth-century farm buildings to the north of the lower lake house the Irish Agricultural Museum where a variety of old horticultural implements are on display.

Located 3 miles south west of Wexford at Murntown. NGR: T 020170. Open daily, all year: 9.00 am – 5.00 pm. The Irish Agricultural Museum is open June to August: weekdays, 9.00 am – 5.00 pm; weekends, 2.00 – 5.00 pm. April to May and September to 14 November: weekdays, 9.00 am – 12.30 pm; weekends, 2.00 – 5.00 pm. 15 November to 31 March: weekdays, 9.00 am – 12.30 pm, 1.30 – 5.00 pm. Tea room in museum open July and August. Toilet facilities. Suitable for wheelchairs. Dogs on lead. Admission: car and passengers IR £2.50; pedestrians IR £1.50. Admission October to April: free. Tel: (053) 42888.

Johnstown Castle surrounded by mature woodlands and lakes

KILRUDDERY

County Wicklow

Gardens are such fragile art forms that few survive unchanged for any length of time. An exception to this rule is Kilruddery – the most complete example of a seventeenth- or early eighteenth-century formal garden to exist anywhere in the British Isles. Its survival over a period of 300 years, albeit with some Victorian embellishments, is one of the great miracles of the gardening world. Visiting this enchanting and romantic garden can be quite an emotional experience – few places evoke the spirits of the past more than this living relic of a former age.

The garden was created in the 1680s by the fourth Earl of Meath and later extended by his nephew the sixth Earl in the 1720s. In the seventeenth and eighteenth centuries the house faced east towards the old Bray Road about a hundred yards away, while the main axis of the gardens lay to the south. During the 1820s the house was incorporated into a much larger Elizabethan Revival mansion by the tenth Earl and the road was pushed back by the creation of a large informal landscape park. Fortunately by this time the old formal layout was regarded as a venerable place whose 'yews planted before the flood' were considered worthy of the care and attention they have received from subsequent generations of the Brabazon family.

The central feature of the 1680s layout are two parallel water canals 550-feet long extending from the house down a large rectangular lawn and aligned upon a half mile-long lime avenue leading uphill across the park. A circular pond just beyond the canal once had a tall fountain, while outside this a narrow water channel (now empty) known as the Stops separates the garden from the open park. To the left of the canal winds a feature known as the 'angles' – in learned terms a *patte d'oie*. It comprises an arrangement of radiating hedges composed of lime, hornbeam and beech with an enclosing hedge of yew and statuary at the diagonal intersections. The feature was once flanked on each side by a bowling green and a maze, but these have sadly now gone.

On the opposite side of the canal lawn lies a woodland area of old beech trees known as the Wilderness, divided by symmetrical walks with statuary placed at focal points. From here the main walk leads to a circular pond and fountain surrounded by a giant beech hedge. It rises from a skirting of box and has

84

cast-iron statues signed by Barbezat which, like others in gardens by Kahl of Potsdam, were introduced by the eleventh Earl of Meath in the mid nineteenth century. Nearby stands the Sylvan Theatre – a mini-amphitheatre of tiered grass seats enclosed by a bay hedge and used for amateur theatricals. It was much admired by Sir Walter Scott who later used it for a scene in *St Ronan's Well*.

The late seventeenth-century layout was enlarged around 1725 on the south-west side by a long, impressive water staircase similar to the one at Chatsworth. This extended downhill from a circular pond and terminated in a pond known from its shape as the Ace of Clubs. It was associated with a series of vistas, all of which were removed early in the nineteenth century to make way for the present parkland. Later additions to the garden were made in 1846 when Daniel Robertson created balustrading for the house and put down parterres to the west of the building. These are overlooked by an ornamental dairy designed by Sir George Hodson, while the impressive domed conservatory adjacent to the house was added by William Burn in 1852. The major Edwardian contribution to the garden is a large rock garden approached by a series of terraces, each one formerly devoted to a particular sporting activity. The rock garden is no longer maintained but nearby a wizened strawberry tree, *Arbutus unedo*, is still worthy of praise.

Located 1 mile south of Bray on the Greystones to Delgany Road. NGR: O 207160. Open daily in May, June and September: 1.00 – 5.00 pm. Toilet facilities. Partly suitable for wheelchairs. No dogs. Admission: adults IR £1.00; senior citizens, students and children IR £0.50; under 12's free. Admission to house and gardens: adults IR £2.50; senior citizens and students IR £1.50; children IR £1.00, must be accompanied by adult. Group rates for 10+ available. Tel: (01) 2863405.

MOUNT USHER

County Wicklow

More praise has been heaped upon the gardens of Mount Usher than on any other in Ireland – but whatever the superlatives these gardens never cease to impress and with each visit reveal new and unexpected delights. The quality and range of plants is remarkable, with over 4,000 species represented including many quite exceptional specimens; but what is particularly striking is the highly accomplished manner in which the many luxuriant plants have been incorporated into an authentically wild 'Robinsonian' layout, covering only twenty acres. A sense of space and fluidity is provided by the Vartry River which flows through the central axis of the garden, while a series of long grassy vistas helps to relieve any sense of being hemmed in by the many trees and shrubs. The views up and down the river are wonderful, particularly from the vantage point of its four bridges, while the constant sound of falling water from the weirs and rocky outcrops adds further to the character of this idyllic place.

The origins of this remarkable garden go back to 1868 when Edward Walpole, a Dublin businessman, purchased the lease of a small tuck-mill in a wooded valley on the edge of Rossanagh demesne. It was intended as a weekend retreat, but before long his three sons, Thomas, George and Edward, began enthusiastically transforming its one acre of ground into a garden. Edward was so taken with his sons' efforts that he transferred the property to their names in 1875. They continued to develop and enlarge the garden until their deaths – filling it with a huge number of rare and tender plants collected from nurseries throughout the world. From an early stage the Walpoles adopted the naturalistic style of planting advocated by William Robinson, who personally visited and approved of the garden in the early 1880s. This form of planting was continued by a grandson, E. Horace Walpole (1880–1964), and later in turn by his son Robert who sold Mount Usher to Madelaine Jay in 1980. It is this adaptation of a consistent gardening style over most of its long history that has contributed enormously to Mount Usher's distinctive charm.

The entrance into the garden lies at the far end of a courtyard housing a number of antique and craft shops. Passing through a gate the visitor enters a quadrangular area known as the Orchard, bordered by a fine beech hedge planted in 1927. This compartment contains a display of dwarf conifers, a long herbaceous border laid down in the mid 1980s and a number of flowering trees and shrubs, including a small collection of lilac trees. From a hole in the hedge a winding path uphill passes a small pavilion dedicated to the Walpole family and leads on to the Maple Walk – a grassy ride aligned on the river. The colours along here are brilliant in autumn, a palette of scarlet and gold from the maples mingling with the striking blues of the waterside hydrangeas. Summer colour is provided by manuka or New Zealand tea trees, including the rosy red-flowering *Leptospermum scoparium* 'Chapmanii', while several conifers in the area give contrast, notably a small but elegant *Juniperus recurva coxii* with gracefully drooping branches and a beautiful false larch, *Pseudolarix amabilis*, whose pale green leaves turn a golden yellow in autumn.

The Maple Walk draws the visitor down towards the river – the focal point of the garden – where bold and highly effective plantings frame the water's margins. Huge gunnera, royal ferns and umbrella saxifrages have all naturalised here; so too have yellow- and white-flowering lysichitons, mimulus, hostas and numerous candelabra, polyanthus and other primulae. Clumps of New Zealand flax, cordylines, bamboos and pampas give an exotic touch to the waterside, while delicate seasonal colour is provided by a happily

Autumnal colour along the Vartry River, Mount Usher

87

balanced planting of conifers and deciduous trees. The views along the river are particularly striking in autumn, the water reflecting the rich yellows, oranges and crimsons of liquidambars, fothergillas, cercidiphyllums, amelanchiers, acers, willows, dogwoods, swamp cypresses (*Taxodium distichum*) and a number of very beautiful tupelo trees (*Nyssa sylvatica*) which look particularly impressive beside clumps of white pampas grass.

South of the suspension bridge lies the main woodland garden at Mount Usher. Disected by a network of paths meandering their way around an old pond, a wishing well and back down across the old drive, it shelters a wealth of shrubs – viburnums, hydrangeas, pieris, embothriums and rhododendrons – while amongst some of the outstanding plants is a lovely scented *Magnolia obovata* from Japan, a large Chilean *Lomatia ferruginea* and a very tender *Agathis australis* – the Kauri pine. Visitors will also come across a beautiful New Zealand rimu (*Dacrydium cupressinum*) and a good specimen of the unusual kawaka (*Libocedrus plumosa*).

The croquet lawn close to the river boasts some especially memorable trees: two rare and striking Chinese firs (*Cunninghamia lanceolata*), a tall and very lovely specimen of *Cupressus cashmeriana* with drooping branches planted in 1875 and a magnificent fifteen-foot-high American Eastern hemlock (*Tsuga canadensis* 'Pendula'). From here visitors taking the Azalea Walk will notice an imposing fifty-foot-high *Pinus montezumae* from Mexico planted in 1906 by Lord Powerscourt, perhaps the most august tree at Mount Usher. The Azalea Walk, a long grassy ride through the garden, is lined with rhododendrons, a variety of fine davidias and azaras, the fragrant white-flowering *Magnolia salicifolia* and a quantity of *Eucryphia glutinosa* whose large white, golden-centered flowers are a splendid sight in the fading months of summer.

At the far end of the Azalea Walk a grove of spectacular eucalyptus trees includes *E. viminalis*, *E. stuartiana*, *E. delegatensis* and *E. urnigera*, some over 130-feet tall. Over seventy varieties of eucalyptus have been planted in the garden since 1905 when seed was first imported from Australia, and today Mount Usher can claim the finest collection in Ireland.

Crossing the southernmost bridge, built in 1924, the visitor next arrives at the imposing Palm Walk – a broad grassy vista that extends outwards from the house and lined with Chusan palms (*Trachycarpus fortunei*). In the area to the south stretches the main eucryphia collection which features clumps of the special hybrids *E.* x *nymansensis* 'Mount Usher', the result of a cross made in 1916 between *E. glutinosa* and *E. cordifolia*. The Lime Walk to the north has an excellent collection of ornamental southern beeches seeded in 1928. Among the eight species represented are *Nothofagus solandri* and *N. menziesii* from New Zealand, both over fifty-feet high. Certain to astonish is a fragrant silver wattle from Australia (*Acacia dealbata*) that was planted in 1950 and now stands an amazing sixty feet in height.

Running beyond the house, a tributary path leads past one of the original plantings at Mount Usher – a redwood *Sequoia sempervirens* planted around 1870. From here the visitor enters the area known as the Island which is crossed by a maze of little meandering paths. Plants to note include an *Acer laevigatum reticulatum* with net-veined leaves, the evergreen Chinese spindle tree (*Euonymus wilsonii*) and a large *Magnolia* x *veitchii* that is a glorious sight in spring, with thousands of purple-pink flowers blooming on naked stems. A lily pond on the edge of the area is surrounded by ornamental rushes – such as the reedmace *Typha augustifolia* – and with water irises.

The Riviera is the most recently planted area of the garden – a long narrow strip bordering the river. This section can be quite noisy, particularly during market time on Mondays, but a walk along here is nevertheless rewarding. Tree enthusiasts will be pleased by a fine grouping near Penelope's bridge: a massive spreading eucalyptus, a lovely golden-yellow *Thuja plicata* 'Semperaurescens', a number of slender taxodiums, a fine erect Lawson cypress 'Silver Queen' and a splendid *Pinus montezumae* tree whose branches trail the river's edge. Before leaving the garden, visitors should walk along the Kitchen Garden wall where a fine specimen of the Japanese banana tree (*Musa basjoo*) graces the scene – always a popular plant at Mount Usher and a suitable climax to a journey around this verdant Wicklow paradise.

Located in Ashford on the main Dublin to Wexford Road. NGR: T 258977. Open daily, 17 March to 31 October: weekdays and Saturdays, 10.30 am – 6.00 pm; Sundays, 11.00 am – 6.00 pm. Tea room. Gift shops. Toilet facilities. Partly suitable for wheelchairs. No picnics. No dogs. Admission: adults IR £2.20; senior citizens, students and children IR £1.50. Special rates for groups of 20+. Tel: (0404) 40116.

POWERSCOURT

County Wicklow

Amongst Ireland's stately gardens, Powerscourt must be king. Its design, focussed upon the dramatic ruin of the house, is on a spectacular scale – lavishly endowed with an extensive range of antique statuary, magnificent wrought ironwork, broad sweeping terraces, elaborate parterres, a pool with a soaring fountain and, above all, a superb setting. Indeed, the vista along the amphitheatre of terraces and across the Triton pool to the wooded landscape and the Great Sugar Loaf beyond is without compare – surely one of the finest garden prospects in the world. Everything at Powerscourt was created on a grand scale – including the woodlands which are very extensive and contain many fine trees; some of the conifers are now unequalled in size and magnificence. The waterfall, the tallest in Ireland, is a natural feature. Romantically located in a distant part of the demesne, it has been a popular attraction since the eighteenth century.

The gardens at Powerscourt are often considered to be largely a Victorian creation though in fact they have a much longer history. The 'manor of Powerscourt containing one ruinous castle' was originally granted to Sir Richard Wingfield in 1609 by James I as a reward for crushing a rebellion in Ulster. He rebuilt the old medieval castle and though this was later burnt in 1649 its walls were incorporated into the fabric of the Palladian mansion built between 1731 and 1740 by Richard Wingfield, later first Viscount Powerscourt, to designs of Richard Castle. During this time an elaborate layout of radiating allées was created in the area to the north of the house, while the steep slopes below to the south of the building were cut into banks and terraces leading down to a central pool. At the edge of this pond, known as Juggy's Lake, an elaborate grotto was constructed using fossilised sphagnum moss; this delightful feature, later used as a fernery during the Victorian period, can still be seen beneath the retaining bank of the pond at the base of the ceremonial stairway.

During the late eighteenth and early nineteenth centuries most of the activity at Powerscourt was concentrated upon the demesne, where an informal parkland was created and extensive plantations begun. By the early Victorian period, however, formal gardening was again fashionable and in 1841 the sixth Viscount Powerscourt commissioned the architect

Daniel Robertson to create an Italian garden using the bones of the old 1730s terraced layout. Robertson was constantly in debt at that time and, as the seventh Viscount later recalled, 'used to hide in the domes on the roof of the house' when the sheriff called. He was also 'much given to drink and was never able to design or draw so well as when his brain was excited by sherry. He suffered from gout and used to be wheeled out on the terrace in a wheelbarrow, with a bottle of sherry, and so long as that lasted he was able to design and direct the workmen but when the sherry was finished he collapsed and was incapable of working till the drunken fit evaporated.' Remarkably, perhaps, Robertson succeeded in building the stone terrace nearest the house where urns and statues of Apollo Belvedere, the Fontainebleau Diana and the winged figures of Fame and Victory stand. But Robertson's work came to a halt in 1844 when his patron died in France while bringing back Italian sculpture for the garden.

Work on the completion of the terraced Italian Garden at Powerscourt was undertaken by the seventh Viscount as soon as he came of age in 1858. He commissioned the Scottish gardener Alexander Robertson (no relation to Daniel) to create the lower amphitheatre of grass terraces and later chose the landscape architect Edward Milner (senior) to design the sunken parterres of the middle terrace. Lord Powerscourt's major achievement, however, was to create a focus for the whole garden – a central perron built in 1875 to a design of the architect Sir Francis Penrose. This imposing platform with flanking stairways and cobblestone pavements was built in an Italianate style, incorporating features brought back by the seventh Viscount from his European travels, including a wrought-iron rail from a castle near Hesse in Germany and a pair of seventeenth-century Italian bronze figures of Æolas from the Palais Royale in Paris.

The seventh Viscount Powerscourt spent a great deal of time travelling on the continent collecting statuary and wrought ironwork for the gardens. The quality of his purchases contribute enormously to the status of Powerscourt as a great European garden. Visitors entering the Walled Garden at the start of their tour cannot fail to be struck by the magnificent gilded gates here: the famous Perspective Gates from Bamberg Cathedral in Bavaria (circa 1770), the Chorus Gates – a copy of a German original – at the opposite end of the garden, and the Venetian Gates commissioned for Powerscourt around 1900. In the main garden some of

Lord Powerscourt's acquisitions include the bronze-painted winged horses or pegasi by the pool, the heraldic supporters of the Wingfield coat of arms, commissioned from Professor Hagen in Berlin in 1869, and the Triton in the centre of the lake which throws a jet over one hundred-feet high, commissioned from Lawrence Macdonald in Rome and based on Bernini's fountain in the Piazza Barberini.

The seventh Viscount was also an enthusiastic planter of trees, particularly of conifers from North-West America. Between 1870 and 1880 he is reputed to have planted nearly four million trees at Powerscourt, remarking later in his diary that 'nobody can say I have not left my mark on the country'. Some of the trees he planted with his own hand, such as the famous avenue of monkey puzzles (*Araucaria araucana*) planted around 1870 on line with the main garden walk. Visitors admiring this avenue as they enter the gardens should also note at the near end a fine specimen of *Eucalyptus globulus* neighbouring a Mexican pine. Flanking the Chorus Gates at the end of the Walled Garden is an imposing coast redwood (*Sequoia sempervirens*) planted by Princess Mary in 1911 and one of a number of very good specimens at Powerscourt – another planted in 1866 in the Dargle Valley stands 144-feet high and is probably the finest in Ireland.

Some of the best trees at Powerscourt are found in the Tower Valley, which lies on the far side of the Italian Garden and should be approached by walking along the top terrace. Among the most impressive is a big-coned pine (*Pinus coulteri*) which, at fifty-six feet, is the tallest in the British Isles though it may be

The Italian gardens at Powerscourt

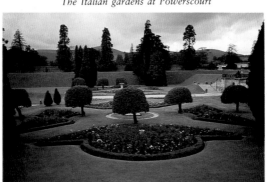

approaching the end of its life; these Californian trees have proved to be very short-lived in cultivation. Here also is a Caucasian wing nut (*Pterocarya fraxinifolia*), a tall example of the so-called Japanese Douglas fir (*Pseudotsuga japonica*), a fast-growing Japanese fir (*Abies veitchii*) and a very good specimen of a Caucasian fir (*Abies nordmanniana*) planted in 1867, one of many at Powerscourt. A castellated folly surrounded by a sentinel of Italian cypresses, known as the Pepperpot Tower, is the focus of this valley. The tower was built by the eighth Viscount for the Prince of Wales's visit to Powerscourt in 1911 and was modelled on the family's silver pepperpot.

Below the valley in a dell lies the Japanese Garden which was laid out on reclaimed bogland by the eighth Viscount in 1908. There is nothing particularly Japanese about this garden but it is a pleasant area with its many *Trachycarpus fortunei* palms, magnolias, maples, cherries and viburnums, although its tranquillity is rather spoiled by a collection of stone lanterns and intrusive red-painted bridges. Leaving this area the visitor will join the main path by the Triton Lake, passing on the right an exceptionally large specimen of an oval-leafed southern beech (*Nothofagus betuloides*). A short distance further up the path is an extraordinary specimen of a Monterey cypress (*Cupressus macrocarpa*) that was planted in 1898 by the eighth Viscount on his eighteenth birthday; it has a height of around one hundred feet and a multiple bole of thirty-eight. On the opposite side of the path is a very large Winter's bark (*Drimys winteri*) which is claimed to be one of the tallest known in cultivation.

Amidst these fine trees a pet cemetery lies on a grassy slope, one of the largest of its kind in Ireland and full of memorials to family pets that once claimed Powerscourt as home. Further down visitors will reach the rectangular Dolphin Pond, so-called from a large iron fountain that the seventh Viscount brought back here from Paris. This used to be a fish pond in the mid eighteenth century but during the nineteenth century was transformed into an ornamental area with surrounding lawns and exotic plantings. Trees framing this scene include a line of Japanese cedars (*Cryptomeria japonica*), an incense cedar (*Calocedrus decurrens*) and a hiba (*Thujopsis dolabrata*). The fine wrought-iron English Gates, which are believed to have come from a Royal Palace, lead onto a herbaceous border running through the centre of the inner Walled Garden. This is claimed to be the longest in Ireland, though sadly the quality of its planting is not matched by its grand pretensions. A line of Wellingtonias (*Sequoiadendron giganteum*) running alongside the Walled Garden is, however, a magnificent sight and much more worthy of the grandeur of Powerscourt.

Other sights at Powerscourt include the wonderful late eighteenth-century beech avenue and, at some distance from the house in the deerpark, the famous waterfall which at 398 feet is the highest in Ireland. Powerscourt was purchased in 1961 by the Slazenger family. Although it was gutted and burnt down accidentally in 1974, controversial plans now exist to rebuild and develop the house with its surrounding parkland into a hotel complex with golf courses.

Located 11 miles south of Dublin city, just outside Enniskerry. NGR: O 212164. Open daily, March to October: 9.30 am – 5.30 pm. Waterfall open all year: 10.30 am – 7.00 pm (winter, until dusk). Gift shop. Refreshments and licensed restaurant. Children's play area. Garden centre open all year. Toilet facilities. Partly suitable for wheelchairs. Dogs on lead. Admission: adults IR £2.50; senior citizens and students IR £2.00; children aged 5 to 16 IR £1.50; children under 5 free. Reduced rates for groups. Guided tours available. Tel: (01) 2867676.

Restored plantation garden at Tully Castle

SUPPLEMENTARY GARDENS

Gardens and Arboreta Free to Public:

Antrim Castle, Antrim town, Co. Antrim. Formal late 17th-century layout featuring canal with clipped lime and hornbeam hedges; also wood with oval pond, large mount with spiral yew path and large 17th-century-style parterre created in 1993.

Belfast Botanic Gardens, Stranmillis Rd, Belfast, Co. Antrim. Established in 1829 and made a public park in 1895. Herbaceous borders, rose garden and formal bedding. Famed for curvilinear Palm House designed by Charles Lanyon and built by Turner (wings 1838–9) and Young (dome 1852). Tropical Ravine, built 1886, contains cycads, palms, pitcher plants, tree ferns, as well as camellias and bromeliads. Tel: (0232) 324902.

Gosford Castle Arboretum, Co. Armagh. N of Markethill. Arboretum in demesne park, established 1820s, contains large specimens of Himalayan and Noble firs, also rare Prince Albert's yew. Walled garden, 19th-century beehouse and early 18th-century gatelodges. Car park charge at forest park.

Tollymore Arboretum, Co. Down. 2 miles N of Newcastle. Arboretum in old demesne pleasure grounds with many stately trees: large silver firs, Douglas firs, tall giant redwood, Monterey pine, original *Picea abies* 'Clanbrassilliana'. Car park charge at forest park.

Howth Castle Gardens, Howth, Co. Dublin. End of golf course road below hotel. Over 2,000 rhododendron varieties planted in pockets along cliff face. Tel: (01) 322624.

National War Memorial, Co. Dublin. Kilmainham/Islandbridge. Remarkable war memorial garden designed by Lutyens in 1930. Restored and replanted in 1988.

Tully Castle, Co. Fermanagh. 1 mile N of Derrygonnelly. Formal garden created in bawn of plantation castle, built 1618, using plants known in Ireland in early 17th century.

Portumna, Co. Galway. Outskirts of Portumna town. Forecourts of Ireland's finest early 17th-century house has Jacobean-style geometric gardens designed by Sydney Maskell. Black mulberry tree planted during reign James I lies to south of castle.

Muckross Gardens, Co. Kerry. 3 miles S of Killarney. Demesne gardens with sweeping lawns and clumps of old rhododendrons near house; woodland garden, rock garden, arboretum and magnificent lake views. Tel: (064) 31947.

Woodstock, Co. Kilkenny. Outside Inistioge. Eyeless sockets of great house, burnt 1922, stare out over derelict parterres and terraces of what was once one of Ireland's most stately gardens. Many fine trees remain: fern-leaved beach, weeping Himalayan spruce, Monterey pine, giant redwood with biggest bole in Europe, avenue of monkey puzzles that is one of best in British Isles. Now a forest park.

Downhill, Co. L'Derry. 1 mile W of Castlerock on Limavady Coast Road. Focus of park is dramatic ruin of Earl Bishop's palace, but demesne also has exquisite neo-classical buildings

(Mussenden Temple, Mausoleum, Bishop's Gate), two artificial lakes, extensive woodlands, two enormous Sitka spruce and small but very attractive gatelodge garden.

Avondale, Co. Wicklow. 1½ miles S of Rathdrum. Former home of Charles Stewart Parnell; planting in arboretum begun in 1777 by Samuel Hayes and taken over by the State in 1903 as a Forestry School; Augustine Henry closely involved with planting from 1913. Has many rare and fine trees.

Gardens Open by Appointment Only:

Beech Park, Co. Dublin. 5 miles W of Dublin at Clonsilla. Two-acre walled garden containing remarkable collection of around 10,000 species and cultivars, built up by late David Shackleton. Gems include New Zealand daisies and blue poppies. Open March–October by prior appointment; open to public first weekend each month, BHs and every Sunday in July, August: 2.00 – 6.00 pm. IR £2.50. Tel: (01) 8212216.

45 Sandyford Road, Ranelagh, Dublin 6, Co. Dublin. Long rectangular garden screened wlth trees and focussed around central lawn; mixed borders of shrubs and herbaceous perennials with raised beds for such rarities as lady's slipper orchids. Open mid March–October by written appointment to Helen Dillon; open to public Sundays: 2.00 – 5.00 pm. IR £2.00– £3.00.

Glenleigh, Co. Tipperary. Outside Clogheen. Twelve-acre informal garden of mid 19th-century origin with sweeping lawns and perimeter of mature trees and shrubs. Open April– October. IR £3.00. Tel: (052) 65251.

Mount Congreve, Co. Waterford. 3 miles W of Waterford at Kilmeaden. Magnificent garden of 110 acres created by Ambrose Congreve in 1965 and onwards. Contains comprehensive collection of rhododendrons, camellias, pieris and magnolias. IR £15.00; reduced price for 13+. Tel: (051) 84103.

Kilmokea, Campile, Co. Wexford. Eight-acre garden created by David Price around delightful Georgian rectory. Contains Italian garden, iris garden, rock garden, herbaceous border, lupin border and woodland garden beyond as well as a wonderful dove-cote. IR £2.00. Tel: (051) 88109.